# HEAVEN HELP US

ALI CRAWFORD

ISBN 979-8-89243-051-7 (paperback)
ISBN 979-8-89243-052-4 (digital)

Christian Faith Publishing
832 Park Avenue
Meadville, PA 16335
www.christianfaithpublishing.com

Printed in the United States of America

# Prologue

IT WAS JUST another beautiful sunny afternoon in Southern California when I pulled up to the school to get my thirteen-year-old son, Jake. He slid into the passenger seat, not even giving me a glance as he fastened his seat belt. I got little back in response to my efforts to start up a conversation. "How was school?" earned me a noncommittal grunt. "Whaddya think sounds good for dinner?" got me an uninterested shrug. But the whole ride home, Jake remained strangely quiet, just looking out his window. I knew something was wrong. I broke the silence again with a tentative "Are you good?"

And he muttered, "Don't wanna talk about it."

I fought the urge to slam on the brakes and find out what was going on. Maybe he was being bullied. But as much as I wanted to get to the bottom of things, I also had to respect his privacy. And I wanted him to tell me. But it wasn't about what *I* wanted, I realized, my grip tightening on the steering wheel. It had to happen when *he* was ready.

The rest of the way home, I played at being clueless, even though worry gnawed at me. We entered our beautiful Orange County home, the one my dad visited years ago shortly before he'd died. Inside and upstairs, Jake and I went our separate ways, me toward my bedroom and Jake toward his. He'd been doing that the past few days, I realized; he was spending more time alone in his room with his door shut. I almost called out to him, but I stopped myself. He'd talk to me when he was ready. Wishing my husband, Jay, was back home from out of town, I stepped inside our bedroom and turned on the TV, letting the always mildly calming voice of Dr. Phil fill the space as I sat down and started folding laundry.

My older son Mat's giant football jersey dwarfed me as I held it up and folded it in thirds. Only fifteen, Mat had always been the biggest kid in his classes, and now, on the high school football team, his size was a tremendous asset. Not only a giant, Mat was smart and kind too. A real gentleman, unless you were on the opposing football team, and then he'd wreak some havoc against you. I pulled out Cydney's petite cheerleading outfit; the youngest and smallest of my three kids, Cydney was our bubbly and beautiful butterfly. Friendly and sweet, she was the artist in the family, too, just getting started with painting. A nice button-down shirt for Jay was next, one of many he needed for the job that kept him away nearly all week, every week.

Mat had inherited his dad's broad build and height, and Cydney had instead gotten my small frame. The middle child, Jake, was also in the middle when it came to Jay's and my features. He was physically more of an even blend of the two of us. Not nearly as big as Mat but not tiny like Cydney either.

Mentally, though? Jake was just like me: full of life, quick, always on the move—unstoppable, except these last few days.

My door opened, and Jake entered. Startled, I dropped the clothes I was holding, just in time to hear him plead, "Mom, I need to talk to you" before he fell to the floor in front of me and began crying, which was really unusual for him.

I pulled him up so he was kneeling, slumped before me, his arms and head resting on my lap.

"I saw God."

# Chapter 1

"YOU SAW *WHAT*?"

"I saw God," he whispered hoarsely through tears. "At first, I thought I was just having a bad dream. A nightmare. I remember running down the stairs kind of fast with my hand on the rail. But they weren't our stairs, not exactly. It was a spiral staircase," he clarified. "My left hand was on the rail as I raced down the steps, and I found myself in the TV room."

My son—my bold, impetuous teenage son—trembled in my grasp.

Holding him, I rubbed his back and urged, "It's all good, continue." And, suddenly, I saw it all nearly as clearly as Jake had seen it. It stole my breath away. I blinked, and everything disappeared. When my eyes reopened, I saw things as if through Jake's eyes as he spoke.

It was all clear as day.

In Jake's vision, we were all downstairs in the living room, all of us except for Jay. Jake raced down a winding staircase to join us, announcing, "It's time."

Outside, the skies had turned red, lights streaked across the sky as if fire was falling from the heavens—as if asteroids and meteorites were crashing to Earth, flames consuming everything. Jake repeated, "It's time." And, silently, as if we all expected what was to come, we gathered into a circle. We hugged, smiled, and joined hands and said a prayer as fire shot straight for our window.

Jake said, "I closed my eyes and…I was gone. But that wasn't all. I can't explain. I just popped up in a different area. When I was there, I felt this warmth, this comfort." He shook his head. "I was confused at first. I wasn't entirely sure what was going on. I knew what had happened, but I wasn't sure where I was. But even being that confused, I felt so much love and warmth."

Jake stood in front of a closed pair of gigantic golden gates with striking engravings running their length and large lion heads on the handles. Stepping toward them, the gates swung open on silent hinges. He looked over his shoulder and saw a never-ending line of people, all gray in color as if they were part of a black-and-white movie, stretched out across rolling green grass-covered hills. Looking along the line, he saw me and Cydney, standing further down, and in full color as we waited to reach the gates. We leaned out of line, smiled, and waved at him. Above us, the sky was a placid and spotless blue, but the stars were visible. This was not Earth but some other place.

As he explained, I asked, "You saw me and Cydney? What about Mat?"

"Mat wasn't there," he said, but he didn't seem worried. Instead, my youngest son reported, "God had sent him somewhere else. He was still doing God's work from before he was born here. He never forgot his place with God," Jake said. "Then I just sort of…popped away again. Almost as if I teleported."

Jake stood on a small mound wearing a white robe. He looked down and to his left to see a man in leather sandals who was also wearing a white robe. Along the edges of the man's gown was an ornate gold embroidery, which also ran along the hems of the robe's sleeves. A brown sash hung from his left shoulder to loop at his right hip. He was posed as if ready to argue or make some vital point, and although Jake didn't look at his face, he knew in his heart that this man was Jesus, standing not far from him.

Jake looked down and saw a clear crystal floor. Beneath it was the perfect blue sphere of the earth. Jake saw Earth's clouds, continents, and oceans as if in a perfect picture. Upon the earth stood a crystal pedestal as clear as glass. On the pedestal were two large feet, which never touched the earth. They were strong and ancient; Jake could see the veins beneath the skin. Worn brown leather sandals kept the feet from touching the pedestal. As Jake slowly looked up he noticed brilliant white robes—lacking shade and shadow—that began just above the ankles. The robes glowed incandescently as if they themselves radiated light. Continuing to lift his gaze, Jake saw a throne made of pure gold and polished to perfection. Its armrests ended in the heads of two roaring lions. Jake could see each individual detail of the lions, including their fangs.

Original drawing by Jake at age 13

The lions' heads were huge. Huge fingers grasped the armrests between the fangs of each lion, making up two enormous hands. The hands were old. Jake saw deep blue veins and wrinkles on them. Despite clear signs of aging, the hands were not weak but strong and healthy. Jake could see the strength of the grip and the quick movements of the fingers expressed excitement and an anxiousness to speak. Continuing to look up, Jake saw the end of a long curly white beard. It was thick, full, and an even more brilliant white than the robes. Long wavy white hair rested on his shoulders, just as white as the beard. As Jake turned his gaze to the face of the being who sat before him, he was met with a blinding light. As Jake's eyes began to adjust to the light, he started to make out the features of the face before him. The face was strong and wise. Behind the head of this being, Jake saw what looked like a deep blue sky with endless stars surrounding the mighty being seated before him.

Original painting by Cydney in collaboration
with Jake of his vision of God

And then he spoke to Jake, saying, "Hi, Jake."

Stunned, Jake replied, "Oooooh…shit." Jake knew this was God. There was a deep pause as if everything in the universe suddenly stood still.

Then God, who was leaning forward, yanked his fingers out of the armrest lions' open mouths and fell back into his chair, his laugh deep and hearty, cracking and thumping like the rolling of thunder.

Jake nervously laughed and smiled.

"So," God said, "you like torturing your dog?" He laughed even harder as Jake remembered placing their dog in the family Christmas tree and other odd spots to get funny photos. The dog had never seemed to mind, and now, Jake realized God had even been *there*, watching. God stopped laughing, everything got quiet, and then he said, "Jake. You are good."

Then Jake noticed a group of people, seated in two rows as if in a Roman amphitheater. Their hands covering their faces, they whispered to each other, looking at Jake and pointing, but neither God nor Jake paid them any mind.

Jake was whisked away again suddenly and next found himself standing on top of a high hill with a large tree to his left and surrounded by smaller treeless hills, again under a clear blue sky speckled with stars. Jake could see people relaxed and loitering, playing some sort of ball game. There was a metal rack at his side, and on it lay golden armor, neatly arranged. Jake took a breath, instinctively knowing it was his. God stood behind him.

With a blink of an eye, Jake found himself atop a high hill. The sky was not its normal blue but had turned bloodred, that red covering half the sun. Jake was wearing the armor he had seen just moments before. Jake looked down on the valley below and saw a grass field torn up by the movement of many people. A thin silver line of warriors just two ranks deep fought against a horde of malformed and twisted beings that were endless, advancing from a burning forest some distance away. Without hesitation or thought, Jake raced down the hill into the midst of battle, knowing this battle had been raging for a very long time.

The enemy, at first glance, looked nearly human, but with horrible deformities, teeth jutting out of their lips, faces twisted and wrong, powerful muscles that were strangely shaped. For every one of God's warriors, there seemed to be a hundred of the enemy coming at them with anger, hate, and no sense of mercy. The righteous died, right and left, heads torn free of bodies, limbs slashed off. Blood sprayed through the air and ran in rivers. Jake's eyes were drawn to the opening in the chaos where the enemy leader stood. Around the mysterious figure, a black and twisting tornado spun, whipping up a whirlwind of screaming souls, which seemed to give the leader a frightening amount of power.

Original painting by Cydney in collaboration with
Jake on his vision of the war in heaven

Jake knew instinctively that their leader was his target and he was part of heaven's last-ditch effort at survival. Jake and his group of fighters were the only ones standing between the monsters and the utter destruction of heaven. Jake knew if he could destroy their leader, the rest would give up the fight and run away. It was clear God's warriors were on the losing side, badly overwhelmed by the enemy. The only smart descent on such a steep hill was in a zigzag, and Jake ran as quickly as he could, keeping the whirlwind in sight. But, suddenly, he slipped, hurtling down, his legs straight out before him as he tried to catch and slow himself to regain some control. Out of the corner of his eye, he saw an axe blade swing toward him, but in a heartbeat before it found its mark, someone swooped in and sliced at its back, making the monster stagger.

Even before Jake saw him, he recognized his brother Mat's presence. Turning, Jake confirmed his hunch with a single glance. Mat looked absolutely exhausted, but there was no time for Jake to worry about *him*—Jake was on a mission. He headed straight toward the heart of the menacing whirlwind, even as people fell all around him, dying, and giving Jake an opening to finally finish his mission.

There was a moment of silence so long that I blinked, pulling myself free of Jake's vision.

"Then I…woke up?" Jake asked, trying to find the right words to explain. "I came out of it? It didn't feel like a dream. It was more like I had somehow left my body."

For the longest time, I felt like any words I might say would be inadequate. What do you do when your kid's just seen God? What do you say? I shouted for Mat and Cydney. In a moment, they burst through the door, knowing from my voice that something was wrong. They stopped short, seeing Jake, looked at me, and immediately dropped down beside him to lend comfort, Mat wrapping a strong arm around him, Cydney reaching out for Jake's arm.

"Jake," I said, "tell them everything you just told me."

And he did.

After he finished and we all sat a moment, stunned, I broke the silence, saying, "Jake, was this what's been bothering you?"

He nodded.

I said, "Everything's going to be okay." I wanted to reassure him that we were going to get through this, even though I didn't know how. "Why didn't you tell me sooner?" I gave him a hug and stood, feeling the need to move—to *do* something.

"God told me I had to wait," Jake explained. "He said in three days' time, you are to go to your mother and tell her everything that happened. During those three days, you will be visited and you will learn the difference between good and evil, so the next time I come, you will be able to discern the difference between them."

He shook his head, clearly not wanting to remember but still wanting to explain as clearly as possible something that seemed beyond the realm of explanation. "I heard voices telling me that they won't let me succeed. I saw…horrible things too…sent to terrify me. There were so many things going on all at once—the voices, the visions, it was like something horrible was trying to break me. To stop me. They haunted me. It was chaos. But then," he said, and I heard hope in his voice, "just like God promised, I understood the difference between God and evil. And I was able to tell you all about it."

"But what does it mean?" I asked, pacing a quickening circle around my kids.

"It's the end of heaven and earth," Jake said softly. "That battle… I don't know how to say this," he said, pausing again briefly, "but as much as you'd think, good always prevails over evil. In this battle? That was not the case. It was *not* going well. The battle was desperate. There were too few of us on God's side, and on the other side, there were just too many."

"I have to call your father," I said. "Let's all go downstairs. Come on," I urged, shepherding them down the steps and arranging them together on the couch while I grabbed the phone and dialed Jay. I tried to explain it all quickly, concisely, and without sounding crazy. It was not a simple task.

"You've gotta calm down. Catch your breath."

"I'm kinda desperate here," I admitted. "Jay, I don't know how to help Jake. There's not, like, someone you can call for something like this. I've never seen a helpline for Got a Kid Who Talks to God and Sees Visions of the Apocalypse? Call 1-800…" I let the words drop away.

"It just doesn't sound like him. Not Jake," Jay said, perplexed.

"I assure you the kid who dropped to his knees on our bedroom floor was most certainly Jake."

"I'm not doubting, just saying." There was a moment's silence, and Jay justified, "He's such a *tough* kid. He never cries."

"I know," I said. "I know. I'm out there on the football field photographing them every weekend. He has never once shed a tear." I let out a long exhale. "I just feel…like shit. Jay, what do we do? What do *I* do?"

"I hate to suggest this," Jay said, the words coming slowly out of his mouth. "Remember that nice old guy from that church? Maybe he can help you, give you some advice."

It seemed like a stone dropped into the pit of my stomach. "Do you think this is the thing he meant, Jay? When he said"—I had to stop and catch my breath again—"is this *it*?"

"Just call him, Ali. I'll be home this weekend."

I immediately began my hunt for the business card the bishop had given me years earlier, having accompanied it with the cryptic warning that "something very big was about to happen" and that our family "was going to need some help." Was this it then? The "very big thing"? He'd made it clear that whatever happened in our family, he needed to be the first one I contacted.

*Now where did I put that card?* Rifling through the junk drawer, I finally found the business card shoved deep in the very back and held it up, briefly triumphant. Then I spared a glance at my kids, comforting Jake on the couch, the three of them wondering as I picked up the phone.

It was barely three o'clock in the afternoon, and although Jensen owned his own law firm focusing on wills and trusts, it wasn't something he could just step away from on a whim. And if I called him and told him, what would he think? I hesitated, picked up the phone's receiver, and dialed the number twice, hanging up each time. Finally, on the third try, I let the phone ring and heard his secretary pick up. A moment later, she'd patched me through, and I heard his calm voice say, "Well, hello, Ali."

"Hi, Mr. Jensen." I paused, pulling in a deep breath and gathering my thoughts. Dreading what I needed to tell him and stalling as much as I could with small talk, I finally plunged in. "Remember when you told us something was going to happen to the family and that I should call you? Well, I think it happened."

He was quiet for a while and then said, "To which child?"

"Jake."

He asked, "Are you sure it wasn't Mat?"

"Yes."

"Tell me what happened."

9

I told him about Jake's vision and seeing God.

There was a moment of silence, and imagining his shocked expression, I realized that just a few days ago we were out in the desert riding ATVs, having fun with our friends, barbecuing, laughing, and listening to loud rock music. Just a few days ago, we were watching our two sons play football, Mat charging through the opposing line and living up to his nickname, "Mat the Merciless," Jake moving so fast and crashing into the opposing team so hard I worried he was becoming more beast than boy. Just a few days ago, we were relaxing in our Jacuzzi, lounging by the firepit in our backyard, watching the kids bounce away their worries on the trampoline. We were pretty much your average American family, with a growing income thanks to hard work, tenacity, and a little something most people would chalk up to luck. We were living the American dream. We had a beautiful house, drove nice cars, and had passes to all the best amusement parks.

Just a few days ago, life was full of excitement and so much fun. Then Jake saw God. Now I had the sinking suspicion that, for us, and maybe for the entire world, everything had suddenly changed... forever, and started to fall apart. All I knew was that we were going to need serious help, and we needed to find answers.

# Chapter 2

MY UPBRINGING DIDN'T provide me with the support I needed to deal with a teenage son who suddenly confessed he'd talked to God. Born to an atheist father and a doubting mother, I was briefly part of my home state's nonreligious minority. Not long after I was born, my family moved us to Texas for the next eight years of my life. The most important thing I remember from Texas was hearing my parents' first argument.

It became the first of many, and soon I'd remember Texas as being the place my father, the brilliant engineer, and my stay-at-home mother of three girls fought all the time. I was a blonde scrap of a child at age seven when my father took me shopping for a present for my parents' ninth anniversary. He'd chosen me, the middle daughter, to accompany him, and I beamed with pride as we walked into the clock store together, my small fingers wrapped around just one of his much larger ones. We wandered through the store, while clock after clock marked the minutes, ticking off the time.

We settled on a large clock hanging on the shop's far wall, and while the owner took it down, Dad picked me up and sat me on the counter by the cash register and, more importantly, a jar of lollipops. A question nagged at me as Dad handed me a lollipop. Impetuously, I looked up at him and asked, "Are you going to leave us?"

He looked taken aback for the briefest of moments but, the smile still on his face, said firmly, "No."

I was tenacious, even then, and followed up with "Do you promise?"

"I promise."

That same week, my father left his family for another woman. When he divorced my mother, he really divorced our entire family, devastating us.

Mom moved us north to her home state, where her father still lived. The house was nearly a hundred years old and not well maintained. Even in his old house, there was no talk of God, no prayer, no church attendance. It was just a creepy, scary old home. We girls stayed in one room with our mom in my grandfather's old house, only being allowed out of it when Mom herself let us out.

There was danger in that household that I could sense but not understand at the time, a danger connected directly to my grandfather that caused Mom to shrink from his touch and keep us out of his reach. Mom said he was not nice when he drank. That danger also caused Mom to go looking again for the quickest way possible out of his house. We bumped around a bit, next moving in with my aunt, then out to our own place. But Mom couldn't manage the rent, so we stayed a while in a women's shelter. Then Mom moved us into another place while she dated the next man, and the next. Having nothing to her name and raising us in poverty, Mom was growing increasingly desperate. She worked odd jobs and left us to be latchkey kids while she struggled to make ends meet.

Eventually, Mom met Terry. They dated for about three months, and I met him twice before they decided to get married. I liked him at first because every time he met me, he gave me candy, but as they say, "Never take candy from a stranger." A Mormon, Terry had us baptized almost immediately after their wedding. Having never attended church, I had no idea what was going on. At the ceremony's conclusion, I was handed a copy of the Book of Mormon and hugged by every member of Terry's family. I was nine years old.

For a while, Terry was pleasant to us, but after my father came to visit—the first time I'd seen him in over a year—and rejected Terry's request to adopt us, things changed. My father was paying $125 a month to my mother for each of his three girls, and although he didn't want Terry to adopt us, he didn't want to take custody of us either.

After Dad left, Terry made us change our last names to his and worked hard to erase every connection we had to our dad. The adoption issue became the flashpoint for ongoing arguments between Terry and my mom, and eventually, those arguments turned violent. The first time I saw Terry hit my mom, I was shocked. Then it became a common occurrence. Mom went to the church for help, but the stake president's advice to her was, "Maybe you should not piss him off."

When I realized she'd gone seeking help from the church and got none, it turned me against religion.

The tension in the house only increased; Terry's job wasn't bringing in much money, and Mom wasn't working. We often went without eating, and even at school, there was no free lunch to be had because Mom wouldn't fill out any paperwork on our behalf.

School was no escape for me. I had few friends and none I felt I could confide in about what was happening at home—there was just too much shame that came with the way we were barely living. My grades were awful. I was afraid to participate or read out loud because Mom never allowed us to do our homework. Instead she kept us busy cleaning the house; she wanted it in perfect condition. I swept, I dusted, I mopped, I washed clothes. My mother, to inspect our cleaning, would get a white glove and check for dust. If she found any, she would make us clean all over again. Beyond the housecleaning, there was the additional responsibility of caring for the many babies she kept having.

Changing the cloth diapers, feeding the babies, there was no time for anything else. My grades suffered. And when my grades suffered, I got hit for having bad grades. My mom changed after marrying Terry; she was no longer the person I knew. There was nothing I could do right, and my mother would antagonize Terry against us, leading to more beatings.

It was a cycle that felt inevitable. With everything that was expected of me, and living hungry and in fear, education wasn't a priority—survival was. Being denied food became an all-too-common punishment, and too often, all we ate in a day or two was a couple small Bisquick pancakes. I tried scavenging for food and hid it in my drawers to nibble on when we were punished for reasons I didn't understand.

As the tension in our household grew, so did the violence, and my big sister, Annie, and I quickly realized that even though we were just little girls, we were not immune to being hit and kicked by our stepfather. The hitting and kicking was bad enough, but the punishment Terry liked best to mete out was hanging.

He'd snatch us up by our throats, his thumb on one side of our slender necks, his fingers on the other, and he'd lift us so our feet were off the ground. There we hung, helpless as rag dolls in one of his massive and unforgiving hands until he felt he'd punished us enough or until I could wiggle free of his grip. Or just, finally, pass out.

Our small house had an unheated cement basement Annie and I used as our bedrooms. With wooden beams crossing its ceiling and a window well that provided a little light from outside and, too often, a space for a creepy onlooker to sit and peer in, it was no place for children. I hung sheets to divide our rooms, placing one over the window so the local "Peeping Tom" no longer had a view. Sheets weren't enough to keep us safe, though, not in a basement where you might wake to find a black widow spider descending above your bed.

Wooden stairs led down from the first floor into the basement, and one day, after a particularly angry outburst between Mom and Annie, I realized Terry—his face twisted in rage—had caught Annie in his grasp. Holding her by the throat, he dangled her over the stairs while she kicked and flailed her arms, desperate to get loose. I slid to the floor at the far end of the hall and pulled my knees up beneath my chin—helpless.

I'd become a quiet kid with few friends, no one to confide in, and no easy escape from the horror and brutality I witnessed and experienced regularly. I sat there, hugging my knees to my chest, watching the madness play out: my mother still shrieking at her first-born daughter, my stepfather hanging a child he'd wanted to adopt as his own, and my big sister growing quieter—weaker—by the minute.

Annie was turning blue. Her wild thrashing slowed, and then she went limp. A chill of fear raced through me with the realization my sister was about to die, and without hesitation, I jumped up, ran down the hall, and leaped onto Terry's back. I knew I was going to die if I reacted, but my body moved instinctively. My spindly legs wrapped around my stepfather's waist, and my left arm gripped his neck like a vise while my right hand balled up, and I punched the shit out of his face and head before he managed to pry me off. My fear left me, replaced by a righteous rage at what he was doing to my sister. He was killing her.

Then he let go of her. The sickening *thump-thump-thump* of Annie falling down the stairs echoed back up to me, and I watched her head hit the cement floor with a final *thud*. Then she stopped moving.

As I looked to my mom for help, she just stood there, giving me an expression of disgust before she walked away. Then everything went black.

I woke up next to Annie at the bottom of the stairs with no memory of how I'd gotten there. Thankfully, Annie eventually woke up and, both of us hurting in more ways than one, I helped her get to bed. I looked at the stairs, and the door was shut; I had no idea how long we had been lying there.

When I was twelve years old, my stepfather took me to see the church patriarch for my patriarchal blessing. I didn't really have a choice or understand what a patriarchal blessing was and just did what I was told. The patriarch was an older man in his eighties. At his home, he led me into a separate room, explaining, "I'm going to give you a blessing and tell you what line of the twelve tribes of Israel you belong to." He pressed the buttons on a nearby tape recorder, and it began recording with a squeak. Then he placed one wrinkled hand on my head and began to pray. Asking for God's guidance, he seemed to try and open himself up as a conduit for something—he said it was God, but it almost seemed like he was a medium channeling spirits. It was a strange and unsettling experience, but it wasn't like I could say no and not go through with it.

Standing there, still and uneasy, the whole thing only took a few minutes, and, at the end, the patriarch lifted his hand and hit stop on the tape recorder. "Good," he said before he walked me back out of the room, explaining that the recording would be transcribed and that I would get a copy. I didn't think much else of it until much later when I received the paper and read through the blessing. It seemed unbelievable: The paper claimed I was an heir with inheritance and blessing through the lineage of Ephraim, the younger son of Joseph (who had been sold into slavery in Egypt). The document said I was essentially a descendent of the ancient royal Jewish tribe of Israel, and if I was good and obedient to the church and lived a righteous life, all the blessings bestowed upon Joseph's tribe in ancient times would also be mine. If I did everything the Mormons wanted me to then, according to Genesis 12:1–3, God would make my name great so that I would be a blessing. He would bless those who blessed me and curse those who'd curse me, and in me, all the families of the earth would be blessed. Not too shabby a reward for somebody willing to obey and not "rock the boat."

But I wasn't the sort of girl to be blindly obedient.

As an avid hunter, at least once a year, my stepfather would shoot an elk and hang the field-dressed carcass in the basement—the same basement, which acted as my bedroom, where he'd skin it. I remember standing and staring at it, the shadows of the hauntingly empty rib cage, the hooves hanging limp. Hanging by its head above the newspaper and plastic he arranged on the ground, the elk would slowly drip the last of its blood onto the cold basement floor. Curled beneath my blanket, I would hear the *drip-drip-drip* of blood longer after it ended and taste the metallic tang that lingered in the chilly air.

With little money for food, the elk was often part of our few meals. But having lived with it in the cold, dark cellar, no matter how hungry I was, I could never bring myself to eat it.

During one argument in my parents' seemingly endless fighting, I left the house. I thought I'd just go on a walk, but as the houses gave way to empty fields, I broke into a run and didn't stop until I'd left my street, and my neighborhood behind and come to a lake. Well beyond the shouting and worse of my household, I could finally breathe. My heart pounded, and my lungs were pumping.

I was alive. I was free. I sat under a tree by the lake and found some much-needed peace. I began running regularly, just a young girl running alone for miles—sometimes up to ten miles a day. I'd finally make my way back home late at night. My mother and stepfather never asked where I'd been, never worried I was gone. Neither did Annie. Mom had pitted us—her own daughters—against each other for years, so I wasn't surprised Annie didn't miss her rival.

I couldn't tell my biological father about what was happening. Terry would stand by whenever I was on the phone, his fist raised to remind me of what he could do if I said anything. So running became my escape and my best coping mechanism. I'd cry on those phone calls, telling my dad how much I missed him, but aware that if I told him anything about what was really happening, my stepfather would beat me even worse. As a result, my dad thought things were just fine. Or maybe he was like Terry and just didn't care.

Even though it was dangerous to race away on my own, it was the one thing I could do to keep some sense of sanity and control. Anything could have happened to me on a run—I was small, young, blonde, female, and absolutely careless with my life. But why shouldn't I be as careless with my life since everyone else was?

Yes, anything could have happened to me on a run, and one day, something big did.

When I was about fifteen, I was out on a run a block or so away from my house when something drew my attention to the small and seemingly inconsequential old home on the corner. I paused and, standing on the sidewalk, looked it over. It appeared to be at least a hundred years old, a coating of plaster peeling in places off its brick base. An old broken wooden gate marked the entrance to the walkway. The place was clearly abandoned, and with nowhere to go except anywhere but home, I fought down my fear, pushed open the gate, and ventured inside.

Wallpaper hung loose from the decaying walls, and everything was coated in dust and cobwebs. I wandered through the empty house, noting the rooms and the things they were littered with. There was still a little of everything scattered throughout the place: boxes, knickknacks, tools, and rope. There was a small kitchen, a door leading down into a pitch-black basement (a door that I quickly closed again to slow my racing heart), and stairs leading up into an attic bedroom right beneath the A-frame. In that bedroom were a bed and boxes filled with memorabilia. Photo after black-and-white photo of people dressed in clothing I thought must have been from the 1920s and '30s shared space in the boxes with old letters, some love letters and some talking about surviving war.

I sat on the floor and thumbed through a box. This place, I decided, was special, or at least it could be to me. It wasn't far from my house, but it was somehow an entirely different world. If people had fought here, those fights were now long over, any evidence of past violence hidden by the decades and a heavy layer of dust.

I began to escape more regularly to the old abandoned house, creeping inside, sometimes at dusk, to go upstairs to the bedroom, sit on the floor, and read the old letters, prowling through the forgotten photos, and allowing the experience to take me to another place.

But sometimes even that sanctuary I'd claimed for myself couldn't take me far enough away, and I'd worry I was doomed to grow up to be just like my mother and marry a man just like my stepfather. As much as I knew that was the opposite of what I *wanted*, still, as a teen, it seemed that there was a dreadful inevitability to it all. I realized there, in the quiet and the cobwebs, that if my growing up only made that fate inescapable, maybe I didn't want to grow up after all.

That old abandoned house seemed a safe, nearly magical place, a sanctuary—until one day something changed, and it wasn't.

After years of abuse, I was emotionally beaten so far down that I couldn't see a way out. I could no longer imagine an escape or a future with any happiness or joy. Everything I did felt futile; every escape, every taste of freedom and safety ended eventually with the harsh reminder that it had only been temporary.

After yet another argument with my stepfather, I ran to the old house, racing upstairs. Sitting there in the bedroom, not far from my house—never far *enough* from my house—I could hear my stepfather shouting my name as he walked the neighborhood, enraged I'd evaded his grasp. As mad as he was, as bold in his hate, I knew with certainty that if he found me this time, he'd kill me. His shouting only grew louder. My heart was racing. From my spot seated on the attic floor, I caught sight of him out the small window, walking on the street outside, screaming for me.

The breath caught in my throat. He was so close. Surely he'd find me.

That was when I remembered the rope. I was not going to give Terry the satisfaction of killing me. If I was about to face the last moments of my life, I was determined to face them on my own terms. I fashioned a noose out of the rope and climbed up onto the foot of the bed. I flung the rope over one of the crossbeams and tied its end to the bed. Climbing up onto the bed frame, I slipped the noose over my head and felt it settle around my neck.

Teetering there, on the bed frame, tears racing down my face, I whispered, "God, if you're there, you better help me now. I have no other options. I can't do this anymore." I felt completely defeated. I was so tired of being afraid every day, year after year.

I had my hands on the noose that I'd placed on my neck and looked up at the roof.

Suddenly I saw a light shining above me, and in it were the faces of three smiling children. Warmth sweeter than sunshine on the darkest day flooded me with love and comfort. Balanced on the bed frame, trembling, I couldn't understand who or what I was seeing, and then the eldest of the two boys said, "Hang on, Mom, it's gonna get better."

Totally freaked out, I pulled the noose off, jumped down from the bed, and sprinted home, not sure of what I'd witnessed but certain there was something waiting for me, if only I could somehow make my escape. Strangely, even after I returned home following Terry's long and unsuccessful hunt for me, no one laid a hand on me that night. To this day, I still don't know why.

# Chapter 3

THE NEXT DAY, I was skipping down the sidewalk towards home with two friends, our arms linked while we imitated Dorothy from *The Wizard of Oz* singing, "Lions and tigers and bears…" Passing the old house I'd hidden in the night before, one of my friends suddenly froze, pulling us to a stumbling halt. I followed her gaze to the house's open front door and the shadowy shape of a faceless man inside, peering out. Screaming, we ran to one of my friends' houses, where we caught our breath again.

I believe now that the faceless man was some sort of entity that had urged me onto the bed frame the night before—something evil that waited until I was alone and at my most vulnerable to try and get me to step off the bed frame and end my life before it had truly started. Something that was trying to stop me from growing up.

I knew by then that my only chance at survival was escape, so I started looking for a way out and even told some of the few kids at school I spoke to that I was going to be leaving. My statement was so convincing one boy even delivered me flowers and wished me good luck on my move. Wasn't my mom surprised when he did!

Annie had already begun her escape, getting a job that kept her out of the house while she worked. She'd made some friends and, making a little money, could go out to eat with them and hang out before or after work, leaving me with the brunt of the housework. I was happy for her. I was too young to get a job, but I was still trying to make a plan to get out. I just needed a few things to fall into place before I could be free.

One night, I lay silently in the dark, in tears after another beating. I may have fallen asleep and dreamed or perhaps what I experienced was a vision. Either way, before me I saw the image of a woman in a long white dress and with skin nearly as pale who faded in and out of view and said, in a comforting voice, that she wanted to be my friend. She wore her hair up in a style that made me think of photos I'd seen of people in the 1920s and '30s. Claiming her name was Sara, she returned every night during the next two weeks, each time revealing a little more about herself until I knew her first, middle, and last name. We had entire conversations all night, Sara and I. I confided in her because, really, I had no one else.

One night, Annie caught me talking in the cold and dark of my basement bedroom, parted the sheets separating us, and woke me, asking who I was talking to. I admitted that I kept dreaming about this woman, explaining, "She's so nice. I can tell her anything."

Time passed and my relationship with Sara only grew, making Annie nervous. One night, after hearing me talking in my sleep again, she went upstairs against my wishes and told our mother everything she knew. Mom raced downstairs and asked what was going on. I said I was just having a dream about a woman. My mother asked, "What did she look like?"

When I wouldn't answer her, she left and went back upstairs.

About five minutes later, my mother came back downstairs wearing her wedding dress, her face smeared with Desitin diaper rash cream and her hair colored equally white with baby powder. She demanded in a frightening tone, "Is this who you saw?"

I was totally freaked out and terrified to admit it was, so I lied. "No," I said firmly.

"What was her name?" she snapped.

Figuring there was no longer a point in lying, I told her—first, middle, and last. If Mom had been able to go any whiter beneath her mask of cream, she would have. "It came in through my great-great-great-grandmother. Don't you let her in!" she snapped before charging back up the stairs, visibly shaken.

But the next morning, my chore list was trimmed down dramatically and, for the next couple months, as Sara's nightly visits continued, my stepfather and mother steered clear of me, barely even speaking to me. My abuse stopped, and my confidence grew. I was happy, really happy. Honestly, as weird as it was, it was also awesome.

But one November night at 2:00 a.m., I found myself swinging on a swing in a park a block away from my house, barefoot and wearing pajamas. Snow fell lightly around me, slowly covering the ground, and the air was thick with a swirling mist that reflected the nearby streetlights. In the mist, white human-shaped things wandered aimlessly, and the chill I felt was not one of cold but of something frightening tightening its grip on me.

I jumped off the swing and ran home, knowing that whatever was happening to me—then and in my strange dreams—was not good. I needed to escape it now too.

Finally understanding that Sara was something dark and dangerous, I asked Terry—the only religious person I knew—if he could say a prayer for me. I had been trying to smooth things over in the house—wanting peace like any kid does—and to be as likable as possible.

I volunteered to help Terry with his newspaper deliveries in the hopes that maybe he would like me a little more and beat me a little less. I set my own alarm clock and dressed in the warmest clothes I could find, and when Terry walked down the hall, I was waiting for him. He took me to a plant where there were stacks of newspapers bound in string. I remember cutting the cord and helping roll the newspapers one by one in the freezing cold. I didn't have gloves and my hands felt numb, turning blue. After they were rolled, Terry would drop me off at the far end of one street with a satchel loaded down with papers, and he'd go to the next street. Then I'd run down the dark dimly lit streets, terrified, throwing papers the whole way. I ran down both sides of the street, leaving the newspapers as close to the doors as I could and hoping that Terry would be waiting for me in his car where I could warm up when I finished. At least until I started racing down the next street.

To this day, I do not understand why I believed God would help me, but I did. It wasn't because of my involvement in church—as religious as Terry seemed, he'd begun dropping us off at church and leaving, so now I didn't go much further than the sitting room, and that was only if the weather was bad. The only Bible in our house was in Terry's room, which I never ventured into. Still, I knew I was desperate for help, and surely a prayer from Terry would get it for me. I had nothing to lose.

After three long weeks of asking, I physically took my stepfather by the hand, walked him into a room, and demanded that he give me a prayer. He reluctantly agreed and laid his hands on my head. As he said the prayer, I began to laugh uncontrollably. I felt oddly powerful over him. His hands trembled and, eyes wide and worried, he pulled away when he was done, leaving the room and shutting the door.

As unsettled as he seemed, after the prayer, I felt a sense of peace.

From that day forward, I started asking God directly for guidance. I asked him to keep Sara away and to keep my stepfather from beating me. From then on, when I went to bed, I no longer had strange visitations from Sara, but instead I'd hear footsteps walking around the basement and sometimes circling my bed.

Something was watching me. And waiting.

One day after school, Mom started screaming at me as soon as I walked through the door. She walked right up to me and slapped me in the face.

"What did I do?"

She replied, "Stop back-sassing me."

"Wait," I cried, "what does *back-sassing* even mean?"

"You know," she snapped, smacking me again and again until the coppery taste of blood filled my mouth.

As she drew her arm back to slap me once more, I grabbed her and hissed, "If you hit me one more time, I swear to God I will hit you back."

"Oh yeah?" she challenged with a sneer, smacking me again.

I slapped her as hard as I could.

Touching her face, shock contorted her features when her fingers came away with blood. "You wait until Terry gets home. If you think you had it bad before, you just wait."

I knew very well that she wasn't threatening but promising, and I ran to my little sister's room because it, at least, had a door to offer me some small measure of protection.

Inside the locked room, I paced, wondering what I was going to do and certain that this was it. Surely Terry was going to kill me tonight if he could get his hands on me. I dropped to the floor and, sitting, used my powerful legs to push my sister's dresser against the door. I turned on the radio, found a hard rock channel, and cranked the volume up to calm my nerves and find some sense of bravery. Outside, the light was bleeding across the sky as the sun set. Night was coming.

Terry would be home soon.

I briefly considered running, but I'd left my shoes by the front door and didn't have anything to help keep off the cold, and the fall from my sister's window to the ground was risky. Weighing my options, I remembered that Sara's presence had been a spooky safeguard against my parents' rage. All I knew was that I didn't want to hurt anymore, and if Terry got me and killed me, there'd be a world of hurt before I died.

I needed another option, even if it'd be the death of me. I did not want to give Terry the satisfaction of taking my life, and I wanted to take my chances with anything else to keep away from the pain. With the rock music playing as loud as it could, I thought I was better off taking on a demon than feeling the pain of being hung by Terry's hands.

Desperate, I walked reluctantly from the corner of the room to the bed, where I dropped to my knees and called her name, and, while crying, I begged, "Come get me. I'm ready to die. Please help me." I was only fifteen.

Something caused me to turn and look over my shoulder, and the room went black and silent. The music had stopped. Standing up, I turned around and opened my arms. Racing in my direction was a dark black carriage pulled by six black horses with red and glowing eyes. Driving them toward me with a whip in her hand was a woman wearing long black robes, her flowing dark red hair streaked with gray trailed behind her, tangled in a wind I had yet to feel. Even though she looked much different than any other time I'd seen her, I knew I'd recognize her anywhere.

Original painting by Cydney in collaboration with Ali of Sara

Sara was making a fast approach.

Suddenly I found myself sitting on the countertop in the bathroom down the hall, combing my hair, with no idea of how I'd gotten there. I blinked, trying to remember, but there was nothing. I slipped down from the counter and walked out of the bathroom without spotting anyone or being spotted. Down the hall in my sister's room, music still blared, and the door was still closed and locked. I grabbed a wire and pressed the button, unlocking it, but even when the knob turned, the door wouldn't budge. The dresser was still jammed against it exactly as I'd left it. Using my shoulder, I nudged my way back inside.

When my stepfather finally got home, nothing happened to me. There was no shouting, no fighting, no beating. My mother never even mentioned the argument we'd had, and I was never punished for striking her.

Something had saved me again that night from Sara, and a strange peace filled the house. It was a quiet and strange peace. Warmth and calm filled me.

When I was still just fifteen, our school took a field trip to an amusement park. At the trip's end, as students began returning to the bus, I overheard two girls saying they weren't going to get back on it. They were going to stay.

Although I'd been wanting to escape my torturous home life for years, I hadn't found an opportunity. Something had always prevented me from leaving for good. Here, though, I glimpsed a chance. If the risk I took was anger-inducing enough, maybe Terry and Mom would ship me off to my father. Mom would never willingly let Terry kill me—as long as I was alive, I was worth $125 a month in child support. I'd watched Mom count the money once, with far more love for it than she ever showed me. If this was big, bad, and inconvenient enough, it might show them I was too much trouble to keep, even for the money.

Impulsively, I told the girls I'd go with them.

Together, the three of us walked away from the buses, and blending in with other park visitors, we stayed until the park closed. We took a special bus an hour north and walked two hours to one girl's grandmother's house.

It was risky and crazy, but it was the first real chance I had to break free.

The girl's grandmother greeted us with a look of surprise. Her granddaughter informed her that we had missed our bus at the park. The girl called her parents and learned the school and police were out looking for us. Once the school was notified, our parents were called to pick us up. Then it was only a matter of waiting to find out if I had struck the right balance with my choice.

Together with police officers, my mother and stepfather showed up. The looks on their faces could kill, but they didn't say a word to me then and not on the long ride home either. Back home, I got the beating of a lifetime, but it was worth every kick, curse, and punch because Mom called Dad and told him she didn't want me anymore.

She was kicking me out of her house, and since I was still a minor, I needed to go live with him.

Even nursing my bruises, scrapes, and cuts, it was a dream come true.

My father called back and told me in a voice so stern it bordered on cold that he'd bought an airline ticket for me to his home. He would be at the gate when I arrived.

"How do I get to the airport?" I asked. "Are you going to send a car?"

"No, find your own way." He was clearly pissed off at me.

That night, I packed nearly everything I had into one modest suitcase. The next day, as I readied to leave, Mom changed her mind, surely that monthly check Dad sent weighing on her mind. "You better be here when I get back," she warned on her way to the grocery store.

I was determined to be anywhere *but* there when she returned. The moment she left, I grabbed my suitcase and went to Terry, asking, "Will you take me to the airport?"

"No."

I called a guy I knew who had a license but no car, and once he assured me he'd drive me, I asked my stepfather if my friend could just use his car. "I'll finally be out of your hair," I reminded him.

"Sure. Take the car."

My friend drove me in Terry's car to the airport and dropped me off. I walked up to the ticket agent, and to my surprise, they actually had a ticket waiting for me. The agent led me, disbelieving, to the gate, and I flew to where my father and his new family waited for me.

It was only after I got off the plane that I realized my dad and I didn't even know each other anymore. He had remarried, like my mother, and started his own family. I would be, again, essentially living in a strange man's house and hoping beyond hope that he'd come to care for me.

Standing there, in the airport, watching my dad try and force a smile at seeing me, I wasn't sure what my future would hold, only that anything *had* to be better than what I'd barely just survived. Because now, at least, whether I fit in with my father's new family or not, I was finally free.

# Chapter 4

WHEN I ESCAPED the abuse at my mother and stepfather's home, I'd seen enough of what I thought was religion and the supernatural to be done with it. I thought the nightmare was over, but it had just begun.

When my dad and I reunited at the airport in Arizona, it was clear he believed what my mother had told him about me on the phone. The first thing he said to me was, "You better not pull that shit at my house." I just kept quiet. Although my father and step-mom, Nancy, never asked, I took it upon myself to babysit their daughter and son, ages twelve and eight, respectively. I also cleaned their house and cooked dinner for the family. I didn't want to go back to my mother's house, so I tried to make myself indispensable.

I was willing to do just about anything to stay. They had food in the fridge and a full pantry—life was pretty sweet. Living with them, at least, I knew I wouldn't go hungry. In Arizona, I also had a bed-room of my own—a real bedroom with a real door, not just a portion of some creepy basement sectioned off with bedsheets. Nancy even took me to get stuff to decorate my room. My life became pretty awesome.

Things still weren't perfect, of course. When I showed up at school in the middle of the year, I didn't know anyone or have any friends, so my stepmom picked me up and took me out to lunch every day. I started to realize that *this* was what it was like to have a real family. *This* was what it meant to be cared for. Maybe this was what it was like to be loved.

Dad saw me struggling with making friends, and, figuring I was a Mormon since Terry had me baptized as one, Dad suggested that maybe the Mormon church could help me connect with decent kids my own age. Besides, Nancy was technically Mormon, even though she didn't attend church often and was a bit of a "Jack Mormon," not strictly observant. Jack Mormons attended sacrament and things like that, but they still drank an occasional Starbucks coffee and knew how to have a good time. Dad clearly thought she was okay. The Mormons were everywhere, after all, and they seemed to know everyone. The church's leadership eagerly agreed. They said they would happily help me make friends!

Although I wasn't really interested, I reluctantly went because my dad and Nancy thought it was best. I also didn't want to upset them and possibly be sent back to my mom. Soon the church suggested I start attending seminary. I really didn't want to do that—seminary required that I wake up at 5:30 a.m. every weekday, and that certainly wasn't something that I wanted to do! But, again, I was between the metaphorical "rock and a hard place" of doing whatever it took to stay with Dad. For the next few months, I woke early, made myself presentable, and attended seminary as suggested.

At seminary, the Mormons started and ended each morning with a prayer, and sandwiched in between were lessons about the Book of Mormon. I didn't really get along with the other kids; we were very different, and I didn't feel welcomed because I didn't attend church often. I don't really know why my dad made me go, but maybe he thought this would help me be a good person based on the lies my mother had told him.

The people connected to the church were generally very nice, but once I also started making friends at school and in the community, those same nice people took notice. When I began hanging out with kids who were not part of the Mormon church and went out with a guy who was not a member of the Latter-Day Saints, the church decided there was clearly a problem.

I'd thought nothing of it—I was finally making friends—but my seminary teacher took my dad aside and voiced his concerns. He explained that he'd asked some of his best and favorite students to watch out for me and report back to him with what they saw and heard. Unfortunately, what they told him was not what he wanted to hear. He then dutifully reported to my dad that the church was troubled by these non-Mormon teens who had infiltrated my circle of friends.

My dad's takeaway from their conversation was, "You're spying on my daughter?" He was outraged on my behalf. My atheist father then went to visit the church leaders and told them that what they were doing was ridiculous. He'd only wanted to give me a chance to make friends, but the church preferred to restrict my friendships. After that, I didn't return to seminary, and I didn't go back to that Mormon church either. Win.

Even living happily in Arizona with a family that loved me, the abuse I'd suffered under my mother and stepfather still had a hold on me mentally and emotionally. Realizing I needed to talk to someone outside of my family to help me figure things out, I went into therapy. I needed to know my mind was sound, and if it wasn't, what should I do to get better? I'd seen and experienced some pretty crazy things—I just wanted to make sure *I* wasn't crazy. I needed to know for certain.

I spent a year talking to a therapist and asking some pretty big questions. Therapy allowed me to understand the things I'd dealt with in my stepfather's home and why those things had happened, but my therapist couldn't explain away everything. He assured me that I was absolutely fine—that I had a sound mind—and my fear that something was wrong with me was completely unfounded. Near the end of my time with my therapist, he told me it was clear that God had a plan for me and that I'd been chosen for something.

"I'm not interested, thank you very much," I assured him.

He responded, "I don't think you have a choice."

How incredibly weird! I turned the tables in that session, asking him about his religion, but he quickly shut me down, assuring me it was not relevant. Regardless of his personal faith, he felt certain God had saved me from the abuse in my stepfather's house and had stopped me from ending my life. God had given me a gift. And God didn't do such things randomly.

God had a reason.

After therapy concluded, so did my thoughts about God. I didn't get pulled back into church, I didn't read Scripture and I didn't pray. I didn't have an interest in God; I didn't feel like I needed him. My life was good. I was happy. I continued making friends, went out dancing, went on dates, went to parties, and even got a fake ID.

I graduated high school, and the day after my graduation ceremony, Dad moved our family across the Atlantic to Madrid, Spain. Dad was a brilliant man, a fantastic person. An engineer specializing in the development of microchips and related technologies, he was fascinating to talk to and operated on a genius level. He was rich and loved living and working all over Europe and sharing that love and those opportunities with his current family.

Europe came with one big additional perk: I was finally well beyond my mother's reach and influence. I would have been perfectly happy never seeing her again. Europe was safer than the US. It was my happy place. After living in Spain for a while, my dad, Nancy, and the kids headed to France. I eventually got a job and a place of my own in Madrid.

In time, I met a man I thought might be "the one." He was an American, and like my father, he was also brilliant. He was likewise in the microchip industry, worshipped my father, and he was in all the newspapers and tech magazines. For a while, being with him was like living in a fairy tale: we attended amazing parties and balls. I was living the life of a princess and thought I was falling in love.

Five years older than me, the guy I was dating was a dream come true. We were having a terrific time. He suggested we become boyfriend and girlfriend, then headed back to the United States on holiday, leaving me in my apartment in Madrid. I knew I needed to figure some things out. Was I ready to take things to a more serious level? I was so young. I did a lot of thinking, but more important than that, I also got down on my knees and prayed. I don't even know why I did it. Praying wasn't a habit of mine; it was not something I *ever* did. I wasn't desperate or scared, but for some reason, I asked God if this was the right guy for me. If there was a God (and

I wasn't even certain there was), I figured I had nothing to lose by asking for his guidance.

Besides, the last thing I wanted was to end up eventually marrying someone like Terry. If that happened, it would be like my mother and I were sharing the same life, and that was absolutely unacceptable. Maybe God could give me some direction.

I needed some serious guidance, so I took a chance and asked the Big Guy.

Something inside me changed with that single, earnest prayer. Suddenly I couldn't stop feeling sick whenever I thought about my boyfriend. I was literally nauseous just thinking about him. Instead of being starry-eyed about our next potential romantic outing, my stomach was queasy whenever I heard his name, saw his picture, or spared him a thought. Panicked, I started to pack my things, knowing we weren't meant to be together after all. I bought a ticket for France to join Dad, Nancy, and the kids.

I wasn't planning on telling the guy I was seeing that I was leaving; it would be so hard to explain. But he called me two days before I was leaving, and I told him my plan. He hopped a red-eye back to try and talk me out of going. He was so determined that he could convince me to stay or eventually return to him that he drove me to the airport to catch my flight. He asked if we would ever see each other again. Although I said that we would, somehow I knew that when we did meet again, I wouldn't want him anymore. I told him as much before I boarded the plane, leaving him behind. As sad as I was about ending things with him, deep inside, I knew I'd made the right decision.

I settled into life in France with Dad, and we traveled and had a great time—it was a great life. But it wasn't meant to last. I was lying in bed, asleep one night, when a strange voice suddenly woke me, saying, "You need to go home. There is someone waiting for you, and there is not a lot of time." Night after night, the voice returned, and annoyed more than frightened, there were several times when I told it to shut up and leave me alone. But it wouldn't take the hint. Strange as it was, I'd experienced strange things before. I decided to try and ignore it. I didn't want to go back to the United States; I was happy. I didn't feel I was missing out on anything by being where I was.

I was having so much fun exploring France with my family and finally getting to really know my dad. We lived across the street from a bakery, and I would go get us fresh pastries for breakfast many mornings. I visited Paris on the weekends, soaking up the culture and history. Dad's company was paying for everything, including being willing to foot the bill for me to attend university. I considered it, but only briefly—I was so busy having fun! If I stayed, it seemed the possibilities were endless. As month after month passed, regardless of the voice, I became more and more determined to stay. France was perfect in so many ways.

And there, I was so far away from my mother—and my nightmares.

I never wanted to leave Europe. But the voice was insistent. One night, my dad heard the voice, too, and came to talk to me about it. I honestly hoped that if we simply ignored it, then it would go away, so I did just that for another month. The voice did not give up nor go away, and finally, Dad suggested that I should go back to the States for three months—just to see if there was anything to all this—and then I could come back. Dad bought me a plane ticket, and, extremely annoyed, I returned to the United States, determined to figure out what all this was about. Who was this mysterious person waiting for me in Arizona?

I was so certain my stay would be brief that I only took one suitcase. Besides, I would only be staying three months—that should be enough to satisfy the voice and avoid my mother—and then I'd return to my dream life in Europe. Three days after my flight got in, I was barely unpacked when I reconnected with a girlfriend of mine in Arizona. Together we went out to meet her boyfriend and his roommate, Jay. Meeting us at the door, Jay looked like a typical blond-haired, blue-eyed California boy with a Justin Bieber haircut, wearing an unbuttoned shirt, showing off his six-pack. A lifeguard, he also looked like a surfer. *Cute kid*, I thought, but I quickly dismissed him. I dated *men*, after all, and Jay was clearly more of a boy. When my girlfriend asked where her boyfriend was, he directed her upstairs. She and her boyfriend lingered there, and Jay invited me to sit down and talk with him. Soon the smell of weed being smoked drifted down the stairs. Jay and I just continued talking. He was friendly and easy to talk to, but I wasn't interested in him at all. He was simply not my type.

Instead of becoming romantically involved, Jay and I became good friends. He was smart, dedicated, reliable, and fun to talk to. Whenever I'd go out with the girls to a club and inevitably get left behind when they ran off with different guys, I could call Jay for a ride home. It didn't matter if it was two in the morning. If something went sideways, Jay would come get me without asking any questions or passing judgment. Wherever I was, if I was in a bind, I could always count on Jay. He was a nice enough guy, but surely he wasn't the one the voice had made me fly back to meet.

About a week after meeting Jay, I got a job at a jewelry store to pass the time and make some extra money. One day, while walking to the jewelry store with my boss, an old woman stopped me and grabbed my hand, saying, "You are special and of God." Shocked and not knowing what to say or do, I stood there a moment, stunned, while she continued, "God loves you very much and is happy you've met your husband."

I immediately thought, *What the f——? Why does weird stuff keep happening to me?* I mean, she seemed like a bit of a freak—sweet but odd.

My boss, a bit weirded out, grabbed my arm and yanked me away. Back in the jewelry store, we agreed it was odd, but she was probably nothing more than a harmless crazy old bat. Still, mentally, I went through the Rolodex in my head of all the guys I'd met so far. Could any of them be the person she was talking about? Jay didn't even get included on my quick mental inventory. He was just Jay. There was no way in hell it could be him.

# Chapter 5

NEARLY THREE MONTHS after meeting, Jay wanted to turn our friendship into something more like a boyfriend-girlfriend relationship, but I was certain that was all wrong. I was ready to head back to Europe, having done what I could to appease the voice but coming up empty. I hadn't had the heart to tell Jay my time in the States was almost up. We had only been friends, after all. But hearing his suggestion, I panicked. It wasn't what I wanted; I was sure of that much. Jay was nice, a gentleman—there was no doubting that. He'd never even made a move on me. There was absolutely nothing wrong with him, except I wasn't looking for anything like that, and I just didn't feel that way about him.

I told him no, absolutely not. I was not interested in being more serious or being his girlfriend. I felt awful.

I'd barely started living my own life, and it was a fantastic one! If I could just live a normal life for a few years, get my feet under me, find myself, then I could consider something more serious. I had no intention of staying. This move to Arizona was only supposed to be a temporary thing! I was going to be returning to my family and picking up again with living my beautiful life in Europe. I would marry a European man and never, ever move back to the United States.

That was my plan, and I was sticking to it! I had to get out of there! I jumped into my car as fast as I could, *No, no, no, no, no,* racing through my head as I pulled away. I let out a breath when my wheels hit the road—I'd barely escaped. My head began to clear on the freeway. I was going to be fine!

From the back of my car, an angry voice suddenly shouted at me, as clear and crisp as the conversation I'd just had with Jay. It yelled, "If you don't give this guy a chance, you'll be making the biggest mistake of your life."

I freaked out. "What the—?" I yanked on the steering wheel, pulling the car over onto the freeway's edge, my heart pounding. Turning quickly around, I searched behind my seat, fully expecting to see some guy there and not sure what I'd do if there was actually someone back there. But I saw nothing. There was no one.

Even weirder than that, I immediately felt different about Jay. In the blink of an eye, going back to Europe meant nothing to me. My home would be here because my heart was now here. As quickly as my heart had been turned away from my boyfriend in Madrid, it had opened to a bright future with Jay. Everything had changed for me, and I knew I needed to let him know.

I didn't want to go back to Jay's place. Instead, I raced over to the apartment I shared with a friend and, my mind racing but unable to stop my hands from dialing his number, I called Jay to announce I was making spaghetti and that he should come over and bring a chocolate cake. I couldn't stop myself! Instead of making a big deal out of things, Jay took things in stride and came over. He brought the cake, as requested.

We talked for hours. We began dating. We fell in love.

Compared to what I'd recently grown used to, Jay was poor. My time spent at balls and chatting up European millionaires was traded away for eating at Minder Binders, a restaurant and bar within walking distance from the ASU campus, where Jay was a student. Decorated with all sorts of strange items, Minder Binders offered cheap food and entertainment perfect for the college crowd. We'd pay $5 for two burgers and fries and enjoy ten-cent wings on Wednesday nights. There were hermit crab races on Thursdays and a sand volleyball court out back. It was a far cry from dancing the night away in a castle, but seated in a booth across from Jay, it was the only place I wanted to be.

A year after that bizarre car ride and chocolate cake, we got married. It was May of 1987; I was twenty-two and overjoyed that

I'd listened to the mysterious voice shouting at me from my car's back seat. I'd eventually learn that, though neither of Jay's parents were religious, and Jay himself certainly wasn't sold on religion, he had prayed for a wife before we met.

Apparently, I was the one.

Even though, looking back, I can see God at work in my life, I didn't know it then. Things definitely weren't always easy for us. We struggled to make ends meet, and things got so hard that my dad occasionally sent money to help us out. Jay finally went to work for his dad's company in San Jose after he got out of law school in San Diego, but he felt a lot of pressure there, and the stress took its toll. Still, we loved each other and we worked hard as a team to succeed in every way that mattered.

Six years into our marriage, we were living in Almaden Valley, San Jose, and I'd been happy until then. We were living our lives a little selfishly—focusing only on us—and trying to make sure we were financially ready for when we did start a family. When we started trying to get pregnant, it was in large part because Jay wanted kids. We weren't having any success, though, and, at twenty-eight, we knew my biological clock was ticking. Finally, we looked into IVF. We consulted with a doctor but decided we would only do it as a last resort. Although we weren't attending church, and I wasn't thinking much about God or prayer, one day, I dropped to my knees and swore to the Lord that if he gave me children, I'd "bring them back home." I wasn't sure what I meant by that. It just sort of came out as an honest plea and promise. I think now that what my heart meant was that if God gifted me with children, I would raise them right.

We booked a vacation to Hawaii to blow off some steam. We had a lot of fun while we were there. There was snorkeling and laughter and a few lazy times by the beach. Coming home refreshed and ready to meet our next challenge, we discovered we were pregnant! I was twenty-eight, Jay was thirty, and we weren't going to need IVF after all.

God had heard me, and he answered my prayer.

As our baby grew in my belly, Jay returned to traveling for work, leaving me home alone for much of each week. My only constant companion was our border collie, Nicki. One night, while I was in my bedroom, readying for sleep, Nicki suddenly stood up and faced the doorway of my bedroom, the hair on her back rising. She began to growl, focused on something in the hallway outside.

That was when I heard it. From just beyond my bedroom door came the unmistakable sound of heavy footsteps, like a large man walking through my home. I'd heard such sounds my whole life, beginning with my mother, but could never discover any explanation for them. Nor could I predict when or where I'd next hear them. There seemed to be no rhyme or reason for them; I'd hear them and then, for a long stretch, I wouldn't. Although it wasn't, by far, the first time I'd heard the distinct and unexplainable sound, it was the first time I was hearing them while pregnant. With Jay out of town on business, I picked up the phone and called my nearest girlfriend. She was much closer, and I hoped she'd know what to do.

Her suggestion was not one I immediately followed.

"Go look around," she offered.

*No, thank you.* I could still hear the footsteps and knew the threat—whoever it was—was nearby. Nicki's focus was still trained on the hallway on the door's far side, her lip lifting to show her teeth as she growled a warning.

We stayed that way for a long time, both of us worriedly watching the doorway. And then, as strangely as the sound had come, it was gone. After I was certain whoever had been lurking outside my door had left, I checked the entire house with Nicki at my side.

There was nothing. No one. Again, I had no explanation. No footprints, no open door, nothing missing. I couldn't understand it.

Our first son was born in Los Gatos in 1994. It required an emergency C-section performed by a doctor who did not deal well with the stress. Our baby boy was a whopping nine pounds, ten and a half ounces. Jay suggested the name Mat, which he'd always liked. We spent a few minutes trying to imagine how kids at school might twist his name to tease him—we didn't want our son to be an easy target for bullies. Nothing bad came to mind. Although we considered looking up some other names, we decided to look up the meaning of his name first. When we discovered it meant "gift of God" in Hebrew, it was settled. And so our first child—the answer to my prayer—was named.

After we had Mat, everything was fine. I stayed home to take care of him. Jay went right back to work, and we enjoyed a normal life. We didn't think about religion; we focused on Mat and hung out with our friends. Even the strange footsteps stopped. Mat was so mellow, so cool; he didn't need anybody. He was the best first child we could have ever hoped for.

Then, two years later, his brother Jake arrived. My pregnancy with Jake was sudden and surprising—it was actually my ob-gyn who gave me the good news during a routine annual exam. Surprise, surprise! I hadn't even known he was coming until he was well on his way! While Mat was calm and easy to deal with, Jake was nearly his polar opposite. He was rambunctious, a little bit naughty, but mostly a good boy. He was so hyper! He was my challenge, always moving so fast. But I loved his ADHD behavior because that's how I was too. I understood Jake.

Four years after Jake's birth, we had our daughter, Cydney. Like Mat, she was a long time coming but worth the wait! We had moved out of the Bay Area and into Orange County by this point. She came exactly when she should have, and we felt ready and knew our family was complete. Things were really starting to come together for us, but we needed a home to raise our children in, and we wanted it to be in a good neighborhood. We were working hard, me as a mom and Jay as our breadwinner, so we felt we *deserved* a good neighborhood.

We just needed the right house to make our home so we could raise our children safely and well. We found an unfinished house by first-time builders in the neighborhood of Mission Viejo in Southern California. The house had a huge yard overlooking the rolling hills. It was drop-dead gorgeous, and the schools were top-notch. It was a dream come true. We had made it.

Once we finished our house, my dad flew in to see it and to meet his granddaughter. He was beaming! Not only was Cydney adorable, he was also tremendously proud that one of his kids had done so well they could afford such a beautiful home. Everything was going wonderfully for our little family, and I couldn't have been happier.

Shortly after we'd moved into our dream house in Mission Viejo, we invited Jay's business partner, Derick, and his family over to our place for a barbecue, even though we were still unpacking. It was a beautiful, warm summer day in Southern California—perfect weather. Our families' older children were playing together, racing all around the house, upstairs and down, while our newborn, Cydney, napped safely on the king-sized bed in our upstairs bedroom.

I was in the kitchen cooking and chatting with Derick while Jay and Derick's wife talked in the living room. Derick paused suddenly in the middle of our conversation and looked toward the kitchen ceiling. "Do you hear that?" he asked, a strange note to his voice.

I glanced up at him and followed his gaze. "What?"

"Those footsteps. Is there someone upstairs?"

I listened for a moment. "No," I assured him, "it's just the kids running around. They can be loud. Might be the way the new house echoes." All I heard as I worked my way through the meal prep was the normal tumbling and scuffling of kids.

"Yes," he agreed, and we dropped back into our conversation.

A few minutes later, he asked again. "Do you hear that? It sounds like heavy footsteps up there."

Derick was an educated man, a smart man. But surely he knew, like I did, that everyone that could make heavy footsteps was downstairs, talking. Nothing seemed out of the ordinary to me. "No," I reiterated, "it's just the kids." Busy cooking and chatting, and with no sense of any danger, I really didn't pay attention to it.

Derick was insistent. "Ali, there's something upstairs walking around."

I thought he was being ridiculous. "Derick, it's fine," I maintained. "It's just the kids."

All of a sudden, all four kids came to a skidding halt in front of us. Overhead, the noise continued, sounding distinctly like the very heavy footsteps I was certain we'd left behind.

Derick looked right at me and gave me the "I told you so" look.

I raced upstairs as fast as I could, threw open my bedroom door, and was slapped with a rush of cold air that shouldn't have existed in the upstairs of a Southern California house in summertime. Even with the air conditioner going, there was no reason for the room to be as cold as it was. Something was wrong. And inside my freezing bedroom, Cydney was resting in the center of the bed, undisturbed, sleeping deeply.

I dove onto the bed and grabbed her. She was ice cold in my arms, and for the first time in that room, I felt undeniably frightened.

When I returned downstairs, Cydney in my arms, Derick looked at me sternly, and I gave him a nod, indicating that everything was okay. Derick seemed to think something spooky was happening in our house, but I was certain there had to be a simple, rational explanation. Nothing beyond the normal made sense to me at that time. Besides, I mused, the house couldn't possibly be haunted; it was brand spanking new!

Mentally, I jokingly went through the list of ghostly issues movies had popularized. Not built on any ancient burial ground. No possessed dolls in any child's toy collection. No murders committed on the grounds. There was absolutely no discernible reason to worry about something dark and dangerous lurking in the same gorgeous and airy space we were raising our kids.

# Chapter 6

MY DAD HAD been an atheist his whole life and then, in his early fifties, he found God. It may have started as a way to appease his wife, Nancy, who I thought was incredibly cool, but she wasn't much of a stickler about religion when I lived with them. She came from a semireligious family, but she certainly didn't dress or act like it. As my dad got older, he eventually went to church with my stepmother. I don't know if he went to appease her or if he actually *wanted* to believe.

I was visiting his home in Arizona when he asked if he could give me a blessing. He had only recently started believing in God, and looking back, I wonder if that belief was exactly what he needed. For my father to accept God at his age was pretty intense, especially since he always believed in Darwin's theory of evolution, and the two things seemed, to me, mutually exclusive.

Then, one day, my dad wanted to give me a blessing. I told him, "That'd be awesome, Dad," and he brought me into his room, shut the door, and tenderly laid his hands on the crown of my head.

Between my father's fingertips and the top of my head something like electricity slowly moved, traveling all the way down to the soles of my feet. He paused and swallowed, then began praying to bless me throughout my entire life. When he finished, I turned around, looked at him, and then asked, "Dad, did you feel that?"

My dad, who had previously been an atheist, grew completely quiet for a moment, blinking and staring at the ground. He quietly said, "Can you leave? I need a moment to myself."

I didn't know what to do. My dad had never been an emotional man, but he seemed to be in shock at that moment. He had never actually said he loved us. He showed his love by taking care of us and providing for us, but he wasn't the sort of person who got emotional. He was a great guy, fantastic, supportive, very patient, but cool. All I could do was what he wanted. I walked out of the room and closed the door behind me. When the door shut, I turned around and listened beside it to make sure he was okay. That was when I heard him start to sniffle. and I knew, in his room, all alone, my father was crying. To hear him dissolve into tears like that. It was mind-blowing and broke my heart just a little bit.

Looking back, I think I should have stayed. I got the distinct impression that was the only religious experience my father ever had, and I had been lucky to be there and experience it with him.

A couple years later, Dad started complaining of frequent stomach pain. We were stumped by the relentless nature of his strange and singular symptom. His doctor didn't have an immediate answer either.

Not long after my father started complaining about his stomach pain, I did a little research and, not liking what I found online, asked him, "Have they checked your pancreas?" I reassured myself by remembering I was no doctor; surely I was wrong with my guess.

Soon after my suggestion, my father learned he had a dime-sized tumor growing on his pancreas. Only fifty-six years old, he was diagnosed with pancreatic cancer. The doctors tried to remove the tumor but discovered he had a blood clot that made the tumor inoperable. They gave my father three months to live.

Every week, I took the kids to visit, all of us boarding a plane to travel both directions. Mat was six, Jake was four, and Cydney was just a baby. Mat would sit on Dad's hospital bed, and together they would build things with Legos. They had a set of Lego blocks with an Egyptian theme that they played with all the time. They grew really close over those months; Mat was such a smart, quiet, peaceful boy that it was easy for them to connect.

Dad deteriorated quickly. Watching him fade away—watching him die a little more each week—made me physically sick. He was still only fifty-six, but each month he seemed to age another decade. I remember my mother called and asked me if she could come and say goodbye to my father. I asked why. She said, "Well, we were married for ten years and we have three children together."

Although that made sense, knowing my mother, I asked, "What is the *real* reason why?"

In a deep, twisted voice, she said slowly, "I want to watch him suffer as I have suffered. I want to see him die."

"No," I told her. "You will *never* come visit."

I couldn't eat. I would come back home, and Jay would see me and try to force food into me. But I had no interest in any of it. I might have weighed one hundred pounds at the most then, and no matter what Jay tried, I wasn't gaining any weight.

My father's cancer was killing us both.

One week, when I was supposed to go back to see Dad again, Jake developed a fever. Easter was quickly approaching, and I assured my dad, "I'll come up next weekend, Daddy."

Unfortunately, on Easter morning, my stepsister called and told me that the hospice nurse was certain our father was going to die that day. It was suddenly hard for me to breathe, hard to think. I was crushed. She explained that Dad was lying there, unable to move, tears streaming from his closed eyes. I knew he was afraid of dying. He would talk about his fear of what comes next all the time. He'd asked me, "Is there a heaven? Is there a hell? Or do I just go to nothing?"

I told him in all tearful honesty, "I don't know, Daddy." But what we were certain about was that there was nothing else we could do. The end was coming for my father, and what happened next would be between him and God.

As close as I felt to my father, I couldn't imagine being in his shoes—you never think about dying when you're only fifty-six. One minute, you're doing great. You have a family, a great job, and an amazing life full of travel and fun, and then, all of a sudden, a doctor delivers a death sentence.

My stepsister whispered, "He's just crying, but he can't even move. He can't talk." There was a horrible gurgling noise from the phone's far end.

I gathered myself and told my sister, "Put the phone up to Dad's ear." All I could hear was the horrible noise of the death rattle, and I knew he was afraid and didn't want to go. It took all the strength I had in me to say, "Daddy, it is time to go. Don't be afraid. Just go." I told him I loved him and I would never stop thinking of him.

Then, absolutely destroyed, we ended the call. Within a few minutes, my stepsister called me back. "It was the most amazing thing," she said. "Right after you hung up, Daddy passed on Easter day, and the house became so peaceful, quiet, and full of love."

Emotionally gutted, I realized I had never told my father how grateful I was for everything he gave me and all the ways he helped me. He literally saved my life, and I never told him, never thanked him. The fact was I would have rather committed suicide than keep living with my mother. He had rescued me.

And then he was gone.

Not long after my dad passed away, Mat came to me and told me that he had talked to God. It was strange. To this day, I don't know why Mat knew anything about God; we weren't going to church, we weren't religious or spiritual, but somehow, Mat knew him. My little boy tried to assure me. He said, with that unquestioning faith only children have, "God said Grandpa would be okay, Mom." He insisted, "God said he'd be okay."

I looked at my son and said, "He's not."

We returned for my father's funeral. I was asked to say the prayer alongside my dad's coffin, and it was one of the hardest things I'd ever done. I stood there, my hand resting on my dead father's chest, and I realized how horribly empty he felt.

Looking out toward the narthex of the church, I saw family and friends encouraging Mat to come into the sanctuary and sit down, but he wouldn't come past that door. Distraught, he sat at the wall, beside the door, pulled his knees up, rested his head on them, and covered his eyes. His pain only hurt me more. Finally, someone sat down with him and kindly kept him company while the funeral proceeded.

Mat and I gazed out the car window on the drive home, riding with the beautiful family God had given me. My world was in ruins. I stared at everybody outside our vehicle as we passed them by. They were living their everyday lives, talking, laughing, absolutely unaware of the stunning loss the world had suffered with the death of my dad.

Anger welled up inside me. I hated God. He had stolen my father away. I had missed out on so many years with my dad when I was a child, and then, when we finally reconnected, I only got to know him for a few years. It was so unfair. We had only started being a family—there was so much more time we should have had together.

My emotions took control of me, going well beyond loss. It wasn't just the fact I'd lost him. I was so damn angry about the *way* God took him from me. He died such a horrible death. He suffered so much unnecessary pain.

For about a year, I didn't talk to God; I didn't utter a single prayer. I refused to celebrate Easter. I was completely done with God. He had betrayed me.

Back home, after the funeral, I tried to return to the normal, everyday things, like cooking, cleaning, and caring for our three kids. One day, as I was bringing the laundry upstairs to fold and put away, I heard Jake in his room, talking. It was odd. It was as if he was involved in conversation, but there shouldn't have been anyone in his room with him. I walked over to his door and stepped inside so I could peer around the corner. I stood there a moment, the laundry basket balanced on my hip, watching my youngest son with his Legos. He was absolutely content, building, playing, and chatting away. And he was completely alone.

I took another step, going further into the room, and said, "Jake."

He looked around at me and smiled.

"Who are you talking to?" I asked.

Cheerfully, he announced, "I'm talking to Grandpa."

"But there's nobody there?"

"Silly Mommy," he said, "he's sitting right there, crisscross-applesauce." And, without wasting any more time on me, Jake dove right back into his discussion.

I set the laundry basket down in the hall and jogged to my bedroom to grab a picture of my dad. Returning to stand beside my youngest son, I held the photo out to Jake and asked, "Is this who you're talking to?"

He glanced at the picture and reported, "That's Grandpa!"

Nodding, I patted him on the head, set the photo on top of the clothes, and hefted the basket back onto my hip. I said, "Have fun," and I continued on my way down the hall to my room to finish the laundry.

Finally, overwrought by my emotions, I went into grief counseling. I was so incredibly hurt that my father had been stolen away from me that I kept crying inconsolably. I couldn't seem to move past it. Unfortunately, it seemed that not even counseling could help me deal with the pain. I was heartsick. Then, one night, I had the strangest dream. It wasn't like any dream I'd had before—it felt inexplicably real.

In the dream, a man appeared who looked very familiar. He did not act like my dad, but I knew that it was. He looked younger, skinnier, and healthier than he did before. "Daddy," I said, "I thought you died. I miss you and love you so much."

He smiled at me.

I asked him, "Do you want to go to the movies?" My dad's favorite thing in the whole wide world was to go to the movies. It was something I desperately missed doing with him. So we went to see a movie together, but throughout the entire film, he never spoke. When the movie was over and it felt like our time was drawing to an end, I confessed, "Dad, I miss you so much."

He smiled at me again, and he motioned with one hand as if to say, "Come with me." Suddenly, we were walking in a forested area in some mountains. We strode up a short path to a pretty little grass hut, and, wordlessly, Dad welcomed me inside. Before us stood a simple desk covered with books and papers, as if my father had been hard at work on something. I understood then that we were in a place of learning.

I turned around to look at my father and realized he was now dressed in a white robe, and in his arms, he held books. "Daddy," I asked, "where are we? What is this place?" He didn't respond, so I prodded, "Dad, what's going on?"

His smile unwavering, he said gently but firmly, "Let me go."

I examined him more carefully then, noting that even though he looked like a younger version of my dad, he was no longer my dad. Something about him had clearly changed. He had a different role, a new job. We were no longer connected in the way we had been before he died.

Then he gathered up his books and walked away. As I watched him leave the little hut and journey further up the path beyond without me, I got the distinct impression he still needed to learn some vital things before he could go to heaven. Maybe they were things he had to come to grips with before his judgment, but most importantly, I knew that although I wasn't ready to be done getting to know my dad, he had been called by God to do something new, something more.

I had been given a message that it was time to let my father go, and I was finally able to receive that message and move forward. After that dream, I was able to talk about my father without sorrow or tears. I could discuss his death, his disease, and it no longer crippled me with sadness. It no longer hurt my heart. I knew that my dad was fine. Wherever that path led, wherever he went, just as Mat had said, he was going to be okay.

Mat had been right that day when he told me, so soon after Dad's death, that God had promised my father would be okay. I wasn't ready to hear it or able to understand the truth of it then because I was so deeply wounded. However, after the dream, I discerned that death was not the end of my father's journey but the doorway to a different sort of duty. As God had promised my eldest son, my dad would be okay, just different.

# Chapter 7

*2000*

MAT WAS IN first grade when I got a call from his teacher in the middle of the day. She said, "Ali, something's going on with Mat."

I asked, "What are you talking about?"

"Your son's talking to himself. Clearly and out loud."

Okay. That was definitely an "Oh shit" moment, and, honestly, it was kind of embarrassing too. It just wasn't something a kid should be doing. "I'm coming down there right now," I told her. I got into the car and went straight down to Mat's elementary school. I walked in, and she was wrapping up the lesson before sending the kids out for recess. The kids streamed out onto the playground, and Mat's teacher stepped over to talk to me, again saying that Mat was talking to himself. Aside from it seeming a bit odd to outsiders, it also was something I'd never seen him do.

I called Mat over to me, away from where the other kids could overhear. We stood under a tree, and I said, "Who are you talking to, sweetheart?"

He looked at me like I was being silly. Like *I* was the one acting strangely. "Mommy," he explained nonchalantly, "I'm talking to God."

"Oh...you're talking to God?" I asked.

Mat replied happily with a laugh, "Yeah, and he's talking back." He smiled and said, "Love you, Mommy. I'm going to go play with my friends now," and he took off running.

His teacher had been standing by the door, watching the standard madness of the playground, and once Mat had returned to playing, she approached me.

My mind raced. What was I going to possibly say to explain this? I lived in Orange County, California—God didn't seem too present there.

She smiled and asked, "Well, what did he say?"

I figured, *F it, I might as well tell her exactly what my kid said. She's a teacher. She's probably heard and seen it all.* I took a deep breath and reported, "My kid says he's talking to God and that God's talking back."

She was quiet a moment before saying, "Oh…okay. Well, we're going to just leave that alone."

Okay. She was the professional after all. I went home, and things returned to normal, except for Mat conversing occasionally with God in his classroom. His teacher eventually moved him all the way to the back of the room. The move was partly because his discussions with God were a bit disruptive, but she wasn't interested in stopping Mat from chatting with God. After that incident, I began to think that maybe, whether I told the kids about God or not, one of them was already connecting with him.

The only time I remember really saying anything to my kids about God was on a day they'd been particularly frustrating. The boys were baffling me with their antics. All parents probably understand how hard it can become to do things that seem so ordinary and simple before having children. Like grocery shopping. Imagine, little Cydney in the cart, Jake running circles around it with enough energy to power a small city, and Mat walking stalwartly along, trying to be both helpful and a fun big brother.

One day, after a shopping scenario much like that, I discovered one of the boys had stolen bubble gum from the store. That did it! Not only did I march them right back in to pay and apologize for their actions, but I also gave them a very serious talk when we got back to the car. It was a weekday, so Jay was out of town as usual, and the kids were all mine. Mine to love, yes, but also mine to protect and mine to educate and discipline. It felt like a lot that day.

We were sitting in the car, and I said, "You know, guys, one day when you die, everything you ever did that was bad or wrong will come out when you stand in front of God all by yourself. Mommy will not be there to protect you because I can't, and you will have to talk about all the bad things you did, and God will decide if you go to a good place or a bad place."

The kids' mouths hung open, a surprised gaze in their wide eyes, and they said, "Whoa. Really?"

Although it wasn't my style to threaten like that, I was beyond frustrated, so I pulled out the biggest thing I could think of.

And, although I wasn't going to church or giving God any of my headspace at the time, I was certain things didn't get any bigger than God.

Not long after we'd gotten settled in our newly constructed house in Mission Viejo, I put the strange situation of Derick and the heavy footsteps behind me. It was simply one odd moment best put in the past.

Until one day, Jake came running to me, terrified, and said, "Mom, there's a man in my room!" I jumped right up and headed to the room, Jake following me as he continued, "He has a big black hat, black clothes, and a big black dog. He's scary."

Fully in Mama Bear-mode, and not even considering how I might deal with an intruder, I raced to the room ready to confront whoever was there. But I was almost as surprised by the fact there was no one there as I was by what Jake had told me. There was no man, no dog, no sign of any disturbance, not anywhere in the house.

I asked Jake, who was seven at the time, to tell me what he saw all over again, and a few additional details came out. The man carried a briefcase with him. His dog had glowing red hollows in its head where its eyes should have been. But creepiest of all, Jake said the man had no face. There were two spots that were sunken in where his eyes should have been and the twist of a smile, but no truly defining features.

Original drawing by Cydney in collaboration
with Jake and Mat of the Hat Man

None of that seemed like a good thing, but neither was a strange man *with* an undistinguishable face lurking around my house. Jake was just a kid. Even though there was nothing in the room, it was still worrying that my son had seen something that frightened him so authentically. I knew from my childhood that weird things could happen and some sort of supernatural power existed, and I hoped desperately that nothing supernatural would happen here.

But Jake was insistent. There had been a faceless man—a very tall, faceless man—wearing a tall black hat and long, black coat, who carried a briefcase and was accompanied by a hulking black dog with red glowing spaces for its eyes, and both the man and his hellish hound had been loitering in Jake's doorway. He said when he spotted the duo, it felt like something had sat on him, pinning him in place. The room became so cold he could see his breath when he exhaled.

He tried to scream but couldn't. No sound came out. He couldn't move, and his face prickled as if needles were pressing against it. He took a moment to really look at his frightful visitors. The man's oddly empty face seemed to lift into a smile as if he enjoyed seeing Jake in pain. His massive black hound simply sat, watching Jake menacingly.

Terrified, Jake finally shouted, "Oh my god!" and suddenly found the power to push himself up off the bed, breaking free, and he ran right through the pair in his doorway, an icy chill washing over him as he passed through them and came straight to me. I assured him there was nothing to be worried about because there was nothing I could see *to* worry about. Still, I had no reason not to believe my son saw something.

Not wanting to worry Mat, we didn't say anything to him about the strange sighting, but it didn't matter as, not long after Jake reported seeing the faceless man in the top hat, Mat came to me, similarly scared. He'd been sitting on the bed, watching *SpongeBob SquarePants* when the lights flickered, the TV screen slowly faded and then turned off, and suddenly there was a man standing there. He had no face, wore a black coat, a black top hat, held a black brief-case, and was accompanied by a big black dog. I raced to the room and, again, I saw nothing.

I decided to see if this was a case of one brother scaring the other. I asked Mat a few more questions. It quickly became obvious that his experience wasn't the result of something his younger brother had said. Jake hadn't mentioned a word about the man or his dog to Mat. Not one word. It was super strange that both boys reported seeing the same thing. The same *exact* thing.

It was additionally strange that neither time could I find any reason for what they had seen. It was pretty freaky. But as the mom of three little kids with my husband traveling for work all the time, I didn't get an opportunity to sit still and really think about stuff like that—there was always someone or something needing my attention. Laundry didn't do itself. I did try to figure out if there was a natural cause to what my boys had seen, but I could not find any, and I trusted what they told me. I didn't want anything to do with the supernatural, not any part of it.

Besides, I didn't want to think too much about any of it. What's that saying? Ignore it and it'll go away? Considering what I'd gone through as a kid, I knew I didn't want any of that for my children. So, even though deep down I knew something was wrong, I couldn't accept that sort of thing was going to be a part of my kids' lives. I wasn't ready.

But life can be super weird, and it doesn't care if you're ready or not.

The year after my dad died, the Mormon church came calling. A man showed up at our door. He looked to be in his sixties, and he said he was a bishop of the local Mormon church. I knew the Mormons had men who were referred to as bishops, but I didn't really know what a bishop was or what they did.

He asked, "Can I come in?"

Jay was away at work, but the man seemed harmless enough. Polite, clean, he had gentle eyes and an equally gentle smile, and though I'd already had my share of issues with the Mormons, he struck me as kind and soft-spoken. His presence only made me feel my father's absence more keenly. I said, "Sure," and invited him inside. We sat down in the family room, and the kids rushed in and started running around, playing, laughing. The bishop began to tell me what he did in his capacity with the church and why he'd come by. His name was Bishop Jensen and, in our local territory or "ward," he was responsible for all the Mormon families.

The Mormons kept good enough tabs on their people that they knew I'd been baptized when I was a child, and then when I attended seminary briefly as a teen in Arizona, they must have noticed me again. Somehow they knew we had settled in Mission Viejo, so Bishop Jensen tracked me down to meet me and my family. He pointed out that I wasn't attending church.

"Well," I explained, "I'm not really Mormon and I'm not inter-ested in the Mormon church. I don't even know anything about it. Not really. I was baptized when I was a little girl—by force. I never even really attended. Every time my stepfather tried to make me go, I ditched." I didn't want to be rude, but I had no love for the church—not the Mormon church or any other. The church had never helped anyone that I knew of. It didn't make Terry a good guy; it didn't protect my mother when she asked for help. It spied on and judged me as a teen. I really couldn't imagine a reason to return to such an organization. And I wasn't going to throw my kids into anything I was so unsure about. I didn't want to force any religion on my kids. I wanted them to decide when they were older what church they wanted to go to, if they wanted to go to church at all.

Bishop Jensen seemed to understand my hesitancy. He didn't challenge my concerns; he didn't try to push me into anything out of some sense of duty or obligation. He just sat and listened and occasionally nodded supportively. I didn't realize then, even though a year had passed since my father had died and I'd made peace with it, but having a man about his age sit there and let me talk? It filled a void in my heart.

I said as gracefully as I could, "I'm really not interested. I don't want my children in that church."

Bishop Jensen very politely thanked me for my time and asked if he could just drop by and say hi every once in a while. He was so sweet and such a welcome presence that I said, "Sure. I don't care."

He started coming by pretty regularly. He'd bring treats for the kids, like cookies or snacks they might enjoy. He spent time with the kids, playing games with them. He once brought a bow and arrow to our house, and the kids shot arrows at a hay target for hours with him. Then he'd sit down with them and, starting with basic biblical stories like Noah's ark and Moses, teach them a little about the Mormon church. He used harmless picture books with very basic pictures of the most famous biblical stories. We didn't have a Bible in the house at the time and we certainly didn't have a Book of Mormon, so I couldn't check anything he said, but I didn't want to either. It was easy to trust him; he was that sort of person.

Although Jay didn't like the idea of the Mormons sniffing around, he trusted my judgment. I told him that Bishop Jensen was a good guy and great with the kids, so Jay was okay with him occasionally talking with them. It was a relief whenever Bishop Jensen would come around; he quickly took on a role like a grandfather might, and I figured what he was teaching them couldn't hurt. In a lot of ways, he was like my dad—patient, quiet, and calm; so earnest and sweet. And, like my dad, he was smart. Bishop Jensen had his own law firm.

He lived in a mega mansion in Mission Viejo, but he didn't act like it. He wasn't arrogant. He didn't drive a fancy car nor seem focused on appearances. He was humble. He was easy to like, and, in time, I grew to love him—and so did the kids.

But, as much as we loved him, we still didn't go to church.

# Chapter 8

BISHOP JENSEN HAD been coming by off and on for a little more than a year when he explained that he wouldn't be able to come around as much due to his other responsibilities. He suggested we might benefit from having a home teacher. He explained that a home teacher was another guy from the local ward. Essentially, he came around, checked in on the family, and reported back to Bishop Jensen. They'd help out if we ever needed anything. It sounded harmless enough, and since things were going well between our family and Bishop Jensen, I told him, "Yeah, I guess that's fine."

Unfortunately, the first guy he sent over was, in some ways, the bishop's polar opposite. Although he was also a bigwig attorney, he was a complete jerk. He got nasty with Jay, saying, "I heard you got a job with your dad" as if Jay's job was only the result of *who* he knew, not what he knew or how hard he worked. He also suggested that Jay was somehow weak for accepting a job with his dad and acted like Jay couldn't have gotten a job on his own. How did he even know anything about us? We had never even met him before.

We weren't going to have someone that rude in our home, so we told him to leave and not come back. Bishop Jensen was apologetic and quickly found someone else to be our family's home teacher. That was how we met Tony. Tony was super cool. He was a big guy, blond, a Mormon his entire life. He had an amazing family with four kids; they lived in a big old house. He and his family quickly became great friends with our family. Tony wasn't your typical Mormon. He didn't tell the stories about the Mormon church that home teachers were supposed to; instead, Tony invited us over for barbecue and chatted with us about his work.

He organized a poker team, and Jay, who wouldn't even sit down with Bishop Jensen and had no respect for our first home teacher, had a blast with Tony. They played poker until the church found out and put a stop to their fun. It was a complete buzzkill for the guys involved—they'd been bonding! It seemed counterintuitive for an organization that wanted more converts to slap their hands over playing cards, and Tony said he felt that whoever had ratted them out about their card playing was an asshole.

Since they couldn't play cards, they started playing tennis and baseball instead. They were having a good time. *That* was the way to get converts—by having fun with people! Tony's wife, Natalie, was great, too, even though she always seemed a little overwhelmed with their four kids. When we met, she'd just had a baby, and her son was six months younger than Cydney. It was only natural we'd become good friends—our children were similar in age, and we had husbands who were often away for work. Our families just jibed. Meeting them helped us realize we had some options for socializing outside the immediate neighborhood. When Natalie realized our neighborhood wasn't exactly what we had hoped, she welcomed us into their crowd instead. We had clean, family-oriented fun.

Afternoons and evenings, we'd throw open the house's doors and windows, cook outside, and let the kids jump and play on the trampoline. Most of my Mormon friends were "Jack Mormons." They weren't strict about their beliefs. Generally, they were a lot of fun. They were our type of Mormon, if ever there was one. It seemed to be the perfect life, but it drew us more tightly into the web of the local ward.

We hung out, we had fun, and we spent very little time doing anything remotely Mormon. When Bishop Jensen finally came right out and asked us if we would please come to church, Jay said flat out, "No." Jay's father flat-out hated organized religion and felt they were nothing but a scam populated by weak-minded individuals. While Jay didn't necessarily agree with his father's opinion, he wasn't interested in religion or attending church.

I didn't want to be so harsh. This was a man who was investing real time and care with our family during a period in my life when that meant a lot. To appease the bishop, I volunteered, "I'll go to just your sacrament." I knew that was the same as communion and that I'd take the bread and water representing the body and blood of Christ. I was okay with that.

As a result, about once a month for maybe an hour each time, I would attend the church service or a meeting of some church members at someone's house. Sometimes, at the service's conclusion, Bishop Jensen would invite me or the kids to go on a social event. It was the social events that Jay would attend with us—they gave the kids a chance to run around and play with other kids and were generally good, clean family fun. While Jay didn't appreciate the Mormons, he did appreciate *that*. Occasionally we would go, but much more often, we wouldn't. We didn't attend church-related events because we wanted to but because it made Bishop Jensen happy. And since he'd become like a grandfather to our kids, I wanted to make him happy. It just felt like the right thing to do.

Over the next couple years, Bishop Jensen continued to visit the kids and teach them bits and pieces about the Mormons. It seemed like Jesus wasn't as important as Joseph Smith, and that was disturbing to me when I had a chance to sit back and think about it. But when we were first being brought in, we didn't know that. We didn't even initially care because we weren't Mormon. We were just getting to know people, making friends, and hanging out. We were just along for the ride.

Things were going well for our family during those years. We just enjoyed life. Every single weekend, we'd drive out to the desert and dirt bike. The kids learned to skim board at the beach. We were having the time of our lives! Music blasted with bands like Nine Inch Nails playing way too loud to be good for anyone's hearing, and we hosted party after party at the house, enjoying lots of late nights and wild weekends.

Most of our time on the weekends was spent doing fun things with our kids—we had an annual pass to every theme park, and we used those passes often! Disney, Universal, you name it, we went!

Weekends were for family and friends, and during the week, when Jay had to be away at work, the focus shifted to the kids' school and sports needs, and the burden to fulfill those needs became mine.

We tried our best to also get comfortable and make friends in our neighborhood. As beautiful as our Mission Viejo neighborhood was, it was still far from perfect. Everybody probably has that one neighbor who makes things difficult for them. For us, they weren't down the street or on the far side of some other block but lived next door. And they were swingers.

We were still working on finalizing our home's landscaping, and like them, we had a pool, a Jacuzzi—standard Mission Viejo back-yard paraphernalia. We didn't know much about the neighbors when we first ventured over for a party at their invitation. We knew they were wildly popular—a neighbor had actually expressed interest in switching homes with us so *they* could be their next-door neighbors instead because, as she said, her "husband is boring." I thought that was an odd thing to say, but I soon learned what she meant.

We took the family, expecting a normal pool party, and saw lots of familiar neighborhood faces there. This was clearly the place to be! People started climbing into the Jacuzzi, the kids were playing nearby, everything seemed okay. And then we realized weed was being passed around in front of the kids. I didn't want my children, who were all young, to be in the considerable cloud of marijuana smoke that was beginning to form. We made the reasonable decision to leave.

The kids were disappointed that we'd left what had appeared to be a great time with the neighborhood kids, and Jake, who took it hardest, went upstairs, looking forlornly into their yard from the bedroom windows to see what he was missing. But it wasn't *Jake* who was missing anything! It was some of the adults.

Shouting, "Come here!" Jake found me and dragged me upstairs, certain I had to see for myself what was going on. Curious, I peered out the bedroom window, standing beside my son. There, in the Jacuzzi below, were a group of women partygoers. Laughing, having a fun time, and—I blinked—completely topless. I had to look twice, astonished. Surely they weren't, not with their kids nearby.

But, nope, even an itsy-bitsy, teeny-weeny bikini would have covered what they were flaunting for all to see.

"Huh," I said, moving my young and impressionable son away from the windows and turning our attention to other things.

As uncomfortable as that situation was, our neighbors helped us with our landscaping in a way. It was because of them that we decided a row of privacy trees would be a great idea! The trees were installed the following week.

During that time, while our boys were just in elementary school, they hung out with some of the neighborhood kids. Sadly, their friends started making some dubious choices, raising hell, taking matches to school to play with, talking about blowing up the school—things that made Mat and Jake uncomfortable. Mat and Jake decided enough was enough and told the other boys they didn't want to be their friends anymore. Unfortunately, the other boys didn't take the rejection too well.

After that, our family developed a reputation for being "better than them," "weird," or "Goody Two-shoes," and we were ostracized. There were group and neighborhood parties that happened that we simply weren't invited to. Our house often got toilet-papered. Grown neighborhood women would doorbell ditch me whenever I hosted people at our place, and our lawn got covered with what seemed to be thousands of pages worth of shredded paper. Our choices to not participate in certain activities and to not form friendships had nothing to do with religion; it just wasn't our scene. We had different expectations and ethics.

That was when the bullying began. Mat got pushed around on the school playground at recess so many times I started going down there to do what it seemed the school could not. I'd arrive with Cydney strapped to my front in the BabyBjörn carrier and do my best to watch and, if need be, intervene. It was exhausting and absolutely unfair. Mat was my gentle giant, and to see him getting bullied broke my heart. I started to wonder if maybe Mat was *too* gentle. With Jay not being around, except on weekends, were my boys getting enough of a good masculine influence to build them into the strong men the world expected them to be? Or was I accidentally letting them become targets for tougher boys?

I decided to take things into my own hands and teach Mat how to take care of himself. After all, I had been a fighter my entire life and knew you can't rely on anybody but yourself. The very next day, I enrolled him in Pop Warner football.

Before football started, I wanted to do what was needed to teach my kids how to fight. I paid a boxer down in San Juan Capistrano $300 to teach them how to throw a good punch. I taught them that they were never supposed to make the first move, but if they got hit, I wanted them to know how to finish a fight.

The boxer looked at Mat and said, "You hit me right here in the stomach—right here, boy!"

Mat looked up at me and said, "Mommy, I don't want to hit him in the stomach." He was a good kid.

But the man was urging, "You hit me! You hit me!" And the money had been paid.

So I leaned over to my son—only in fourth grade at the time—and said, "Mat, I just paid that man three hundred dollars for this. You go hit that man in the stomach."

While Mat hesitated, Jake was jumping all around, volunteering, "I'll do it! I'll do it!" Like always, my ADHD boy was all over it, eager and happy to give it a try.

I also decided to round out the boys' time with wrestling, doing my best to make sure my boys could handle schoolyard threats. Always big for his age, Mat got put to use by the coach as his "testing dummy" to help him demonstrate new holds and moves. The boys participated for a while, but eventually, Mat came to me and said, "Mom, I don't think I want to do this anymore."

"Why?"

"How we have to grab each other makes me feel uncomfortable."

"That's fair, I get it." Even though I was always there, watching everything, I could see how things could definitely be uncomfortable, and I was trying to make my boys feel stronger and better about things, not worse, so wrestling was short-lived.

The bullies were not daunted by word of what my kids were doing and, one day, they showed up in our yard when Jake was outside. Jake was young and small—an easy target. The bullies caught him, and the oldest and biggest of their group pounded the crap out of him. Mat, my gentle giant, realized what was happening and went straight out there, grabbed the biggest one, and beat the living daylights out of him, sending all the other boys running. Three hundred dollars was a small price to pay for what Mat had learned to do and the knowledge that my boys were now safer in the neighborhood. Our standards were high, and I wanted to emulate the way my dad had lived his life. No bullying, no drama, just good times.

Wanting my boys to grow up as real rough-and-tumble American boys—even though Jay was seldom around—I was excited for them to join Pop Warner football. To support their efforts and be as involved as possible, I became the team photographer. I was on the field with the coaches and on the sideline with the team, taking picture after picture and making memories.

During those fantastic early years, God was barely ever on our minds, and even when he was, he was a passing thought. I had no idea then how important God's presence would be for my family— and how absolutely life-changing.

# Chapter 9

EVEN THOUGH GOD wasn't on my mind at the time, he still managed to be a presence in my children's lives. When Cydney was about three or four, I remember seeing her standing in the yard, wearing her Cinderella sunglasses and peering up at the sky. She was adorable, and after I watched her examining the brightest part of the sky for a minute or two, I asked her what she was doing. With the same matter-of-fact attitude Mat had given me about talking to God, she simply opened her arms wide and explained, "God is in the sun."

I thought little of it—she wasn't much more than a baby, after all, and was just being silly in that innocent way kids are. It quickly became just a funny anecdote, but now, looking back, the memory makes me wonder why she thought to connect God to light and the sun when she was so young.

Cydney's early acknowledgment of God's presence in her life wasn't the only supernatural connection she experienced as a young girl. In 2005, when Cydney was about five years old, she was sitting on my bed one night while I was downstairs, packing Mat's and Jake's lunches for the next day. Something strange in the hall outside caught Cydney's attention. Beyond the bedroom's open doorway, at the hall's far end, was a table displaying a few family photos. Beside the table stood a stranger in a polka-dot dress—a woman—dressed in clothes from a different time period, her hair curled and styled in an old-fashioned updo. The woman, cast in a bluish hue, was examining each of the photos. Then, as if she realized she was being watched, she turned and looked at Cydney. She smiled. Then she continued down the hall and was gone, taking the blue glow of light with her.

When Bishop showed up at my door one day in 2006, I wasn't surprised. Even though Tony had taken over the role of being the Mormon church's main representative in our house as our family's home teacher, Bishop still occasionally stopped by. I was ready to call the kids and have them sit down with him, but he looked at me with great seriousness and said he only wanted to speak to me.

We walked into the living room together, and he said, "I think you'd better sit down for this, Ali," and, although I thought that was strange, I took a seat on the couch across from him and waited for him to speak. "I'm leaving my role as bishop," he said.

"What?"

Smiling, he explained bishops only stayed in that role for a certain amount of time, and as his time in that capacity was soon coming to an end, it was common for bishops to pray and ask for guidance before leaving their office so they could tie off any loose ends. Bishop said he had gotten on his knees, as he had done numerous times, and began praying when a disturbing feeling came across him. He said, "As I was praying, I felt that something very bad was going to happen to the ward and, for some reason, you would be involved." He explained, "I was given a foreboding sensation to try and protect you from the bad things that will happen. I had a powerful feeling that something big was about to happen to your family." In a stern voice, he warned, "When that big thing happens, you need to come to me and let me know."

"What sort of thing?"

"I don't know." He pulled out a business card and slid it across the coffee table to me. "That's my office," he explained. "When it happens, call me immediately, you understand?"

"When *what* happens?" I tried again. I thought that, as sweet as he was, he was acting a little crazy. I knew he wasn't a liar, but what on earth could he be so concerned about?

"You'll know what it is when it happens," he assured me.

This was some sort of hocus-pocus! What Bishop was saying wasn't like anything he had ever said before. Was he losing his mind? "Do we have some kind of a time frame?" I asked.

He shook his head. "I don't know when, and I don't know what, but it will be significant. You know as much as I do about this now," he said, getting to his feet again.

"Okay," I said, walking him to the door, the business card still in my hand. I wasn't sure what to say as he readied to go to his car. I managed a "Thanks," holding up the business card.

He nodded gravely, got into his car, and drove away.

I glanced at the card. How weird. He seemed so intent about… whatever it was. I walked over to the desk, opened the drawer, and tossed the card inside.

One time, Jay and I, in support of our home teacher, Tony, and his wife, Natalie, attended what they called a "fireside" or "get-together" in a church member's home. The Mormon church liked to blend social and religious events together to help bond and grow the community. Although we didn't really attend such things, we briefly stopped by before going to a dinner reservation with our friends. So there we were, sitting together and looking forward to our evening out, when the church members were invited to get up individually and discuss any concerns they had about living in our modern society. At that point, a woman stood up and boldly proclaimed, "Satan stands on every corner!"

I was taken aback and looked at Jay, who seemed just as surprised as I was. What threat had this woman identified that we had somehow overlooked? I tried to figure out what on earth she was talking about as she rambled on about how Satan was tempting everyone and pretty much everywhere, while never really nailing down what she meant by Satan.

Always having been a bit of a smart-ass, I said loudly, "Are we talking about prostitution?"

Others around me started to giggle, but the speaker just stood there, staring at me with her lips pressed tightly together, completely pissed off.

She said, "No! It's Starbucks… It's *Starbucks!*" she raged, imply-ing that Starbucks was the devil's helper and was on every corner, tempting us. To her, Starbucks was the devil.

To Jay and me, that was absurd. Over the top. If the message she'd gotten from her church was that Starbucks was a threat to peo-ple's souls—if a coffee shop inspired such rage—what reaction would the church support when dealing with bigger issues?

She continued telling the group, "The magazines at the grocery checkout are porn." Magazines displayed at the end of the aisle lead-ing to the cash register like *Ladies' Home Journal, People*, and *Taste of Home* were somehow pornography. And we had no idea! How naive of us! By this point, I was hitting Jay, and we were just dying; we were laughing so hard! All of these strict Mormons sitting around us, trying to be serious—even as stunned as they had to be—and we just had to laugh.

It was all so bizarre! But as weird as it was and as tempting as it was to dismiss one woman's outrage as odd or kooky, maybe we should have considered it a warning of things to come. If this church, this ward, didn't question or correct such over-the-top views, what sort of message and guidance was it giving? What strange behaviors among the congregation members were acceptable or even encouraged?

Of the few church-related things we tried during those years in Mission Viejo, there was a meeting Jay attended. Going to it was like doing a favor for both Bishop and Tony, only it didn't go the way he expected, and when he came home later, he surprised me with what he had learned.

"So how was the church meeting?" I asked, sitting down on the couch with him.

"It was strange," Jay began. "They had a bunch of us sitting in the gym on these folding chairs and started talking about how the Mormon church was investing in a strategy that would help them attract new members."

"Are they having that much trouble getting new people to join? Why?" I could see the disbelief in Jay's expression. He already doubted the very existence of God, but to then have people keep screwing up moments when he might find a reason to believe? No church or religion would win him over that way.

He nodded. "You wouldn't believe it! They actually hired non-Mormon consultants, Ali."

"Consultants?"

"They were asking if we know any movie stars or wealthy people to help the brand."

"Yeah. I mean, if the church is true, if its message is correct and they already have a prophet with a direct line to God, why do they need guys with marketing degrees to tell them what to say? They're rebranding Mormonism," I said. "Something must be wrong."

"Exactly. If you have to hire somebody to teach you how to convince others your religion's right—" He shook his head again. "It just feels more like a business than a church. I have no interest in going back."

"I understand," I said, and I did. I had no love for the Mormons, and I agreed. Jay raised an excellent point. If the church was true and had God speaking directly to its prophet, why did they need to go shopping for expert help to put out his message?

Not long after Jay expressed his concerns about the church's method of putting together its message for the masses, our home teacher, Tony, showed up at our door, distraught. His eyes were red and wet with tears, and he was more emotional than I'd ever seen him.

Over time, Tony and his wife, Natalie, became friends of ours. We were considered "investigators" in the church and were essentially shopping around to see if the Mormon way was a good fit for our family. As investigators, we were invited to participate in many church-related activities, but we weren't yet obligated to anything.

Tony, Natalie, and their family were a great group to make investigators like us feel welcome and comfortable. They tried hard and were great to be around. To see him so upset was troubling.

"What's going on? Come, sit down."

Joining us, he said, "I just found out I'm no longer your family's home teacher." Tony shot out, "What did I do wrong? Why did you guys release me? I thought we were friends."

"What?" I had no idea what he was talking about. "We are friends, I don't understand what's going on."

"The only way I can be released as your home teacher is if you requested it," he stated.

"No, absolutely not. We would never do that." I was equally confused.

"This never happens," Tony specified. "The Mormon church doesn't do this. Home teachers are assigned for—" Words failed him. "A decade or two," he finally said. "I need to understand why this has happened. I'm so confused."

"I'll get to the bottom of this. I'll call Bishop." Surely he'd know and be able to explain it to us. "I swear we did not request this. We love you and your family."

With enough assurances to bolster him, Tony headed home, and I got on the phone.

Bishop picked up immediately. "Tony was just here," I explained, "upset that he's no longer our home teacher. What's going on?"

Bishop heaved out a sigh. "He's going to be involved in something bad that's about to happen, and I have to trust him. So for your family's safety, I pulled Tony, and I want you all as far away from him and his family as possible. Do not communicate with him, do not have him over to your home."

We were barely even involved in the church at the time. Yes, we occasionally had done Bishop a solid and attended something—as a show of support for him and his good work and to show his peers he was not wasting time—but mostly, when it wasn't time for school or sports, we were out having a blast in the desert. We were having a lot of fun away from the Mormons. We weren't going to have our family indoctrinated into any church by being steeped in its preaching or prayers. We were well out on the church's fringe. It felt good.

Don't get me wrong—our family was always very proper: we were polite, honest, dressed modestly, and never made a scene in public. We believed firmly in talking things out, and even when we were occasionally uncomfortable with people, we still smiled and tried to be kind. But as proper as we were, every weekend with us was much more *party* than it ever was *prayer*.

To think that, because Tony was going to be in some sort of church-related trouble, our family could be in danger, it was mind-blowing. Besides, Tony and his family had become like an extension of *our* family.

"Are you kidding me?" I asked. "He's our friend. We're more than just that home teacher thing that you guys do. We're really good friends," I insisted.

"You have to trust me."

How crazy! But Bishop had never steered us wrong before, and I knew in my heart he was a good man. An honest man. Whether or not the church was true, Bishop was, and I took his words to heart, even when he suddenly said, "I need to baptize your children. It's important that your children be baptized in case anything should happen to them. They need to be protected."

My heart thumped against my rib cage. *What* might happen to my children?

He continued, his words more passionate now, "I know you have a problem with the Mormon church, Ali, but no matter what, those children need to be baptized. It's not about the church, whether it's Mormon or something else, it's all about the baptism. Baptism brings the Holy Spirit. It does not matter what religion, your children need the power of the Holy Spirit for what is to come. I'll do it myself. It doesn't need to even be in the church. Your swimming pool, whatever, so long as they're baptized."

He made sense and had a compelling argument. "I'll talk to Jay and the kids," I said.

"You do that, Ali. I'll call you tomorrow."

Our world seemed to be tipping. We'd just been told something big was going to happen to our family, but we had no idea what, when, or how. How could we possibly prepare for something like that? Bishop was leaving his role as our ward's bishop, and our home teacher was being pulled away from our family. The people we had connected to and felt comfortable with seemed to be disappearing. On top of all that, Jay was wondering what was so wrong that the church was rebranding, and now we needed to get the kids baptized? In case something should happen to them? My head was spinning. It was a lot to take in.

# Chapter 10

OUR FAMILY DISCUSSED the idea of baptism, and although we didn't really know what it meant to be baptized, it didn't seem like it would hurt anyone in any way, so we decided to go through with it. Unfortunately, when I gave Bishop the good news, he already had one foot out the door and was heading off on a lengthy family vacation before being officially released from his role in our ward. He said he'd be back in about three weeks, and then he would baptize the kids.

I said, "Okay," because what else was there to say, really?

For the next few weeks, we went back to our normal family routine and didn't give much thought to God or the church or baptism. When Bishop returned from his vacation, he was adamant that he be the one to baptize the kids. But as we were starting to prepare, he got word that his daughter in Utah had fallen off her horse and shattered her leg. She needed help, and like any good father would, Bishop sprang into action, he and his wife heading out to take care of her and her three kids. As a result, Bishop was gone for another few weeks.

While Bishop was away, Tony came back by. He wanted to ask Jay for advice as a lawyer. Jay and I both knew what Bishop had said about steering clear of Tony and his entire family, but how do you turn away a friend when they clearly need you?

We sat down together, and Tony told us about an embezzlement scandal of massive proportions associated with the church that he'd uncovered. It all started because a man whose wife was a member of the church had begun a special nonprofit foundation called the Allure Foundation. Although the man's wife was a Mormon, neither he nor his children were, which meant he did not need to pay a tithe.

While most churches sent around offering plates at Sunday service for people to drop money into, some pushed paying the church a tithe of 10 percent of your income. The money ward members made was very much the business of the church, and if you didn't pay your 10 percent, you could lose your Temple Recommend.

A Mormon Temple Recommend was a membership card of sorts that proved you were in good enough standing with the Church of Latter-Day Saints that you could enter the temple and participate in sacred ceremonies there. Like weddings. In order for a family to be together in heaven, they had to be married in the temple and keep their Temple Recommend, or so we were told. The loss of a Temple Recommend kept your family from being eternally connected in the afterlife as, without a Temple Recommend, you could not be in good standing with the church, and you weren't considered to be in good standing with God either. And, obviously, to be admitted to heaven or the celestial kingdom, you needed to be in good standing with God.

We were told a Temple Recommend had serious influence over where you wound up at the end of your life. If you were a member of the LDS, you wanted to earn a Recommend and keep it, and that meant paying your dues. The earning and maintaining of that precious Recommend—and fear of its loss—helped keep members in line, pay their tithe, and do whatever the church instructed. On top of tithing, once a month, they had Fast Sunday when the young men of the church went to the members' houses and asked for a fast tithe on top of the regular 10 percent tithe.

When your family's souls are essentially being held hostage by your obedience to your ward, you tend to fall in line.

The church really wanted to bring the wealthy husband and the couple's kids in as members because a significant tithe would be paid, and, as Jay had seen at the priesthood meeting, members were definitely desired.

To make the church more attractive to Allure's founder, the ward leadership started talking the foundation up.

It was starting to sound like the message the ward was sending was connected more to a collection of cash than to Christ, and it seemed your soul's final destination was determined by what men in leadership judged to be your place in their world and your worthiness to have a Temple Recommend. Did you really need the approval of men to connect to God?

If you had the money to invest, the church made it sound like it was a no-brainer since it would allow investors to build business connections. Some people, though, wanted more of a commitment from the Allure Foundation's founder, so he got baptized, and the money started rolling in for him, and he and the new bishop became close.

Jay and I weren't impressed how money bought influence within the church. It was easy to identify cliques, and the more money you had, the more power you could wield. Jay and I had both lived frugally from time to time, so we were pretty comfortable with people from different economic backgrounds. We were fine being friends with anyone who seemed friendly.

Lots of other ward members, though, including Tony, invested to build more business-related connections. By itself, Tony's investment might not have been a problem, but someone tipped him off about the foundation being a shell corporation. He discovered what looked to be an embezzling scheme. Tony explained that the whole organization was a scam, and the church—the bishop replacing Bishop Jensen—was singing its praises. When Tony found out about the embezzlement, he decided to act.

In the Mormon religion, you don't take your problems to outside authorities—you take it to your bishop. It is Mormon policy to keep information told to them confidential from anyone who was not a higher-up or part of the bishop's team.

Tony explained to us that the moment he had found out about the embezzlement, he raced to the new bishop and spilled everything he'd found out. That night, the Allure Foundation owner showed up to Tony's house and confronted him, screaming. He'd done exactly what the church taught its members to do, and he was betrayed.

Overnight, everything Tony worked for in the Mormon church disappeared. People stopped going to his social events. He and his family were ostracized and excluded from the ward. When Tony confronted the new bishop about his clear lack of confidentiality, the bishop sided with his friends at the Allure Foundation. More than that, he blamed Tony for poking his nose into other people's business.

Tony hired a private investigator to scrutinize the Allure Foundation. When the new bishop and creator of the Allure Foundation found out, it brought a civil war to the ward. The members of the ward quickly picked sides, and fighting broke out in the halls of the church.

The new bishop was furious at Tony, and Tony's family paid the price. It was church-sanctioned cruelty, something I'd never thought the Mormon church would be capable of. Even though I didn't know much about Mormonism or any religion, really, I was fairly certain the behaviors we saw exhibited by church members were not the behaviors of good Christians.

Despite the increasing persecution, Tony could not walk away from the scandal. He and his wife, Natalie, and especially his children, bore the brunt of it. Natalie, a true believer of the Mormon faith, could not handle being both shunned and taunted by the Mormon church members and the ward leadership. Her church became her own personal hell. Beginning with the birth of their most recent child, she clearly struggled with postpartum and depression, but, even when she was sad, I loved her. I knew we all went through hard times occasionally. Unfortunately, Natalie was about to be socked by much more than the already heavy weight of motherhood.

One day she called me, crying. She told me she was being relentlessly harassed. While she and her children waited at the bus stop, the ward's Mormon wives found and harassed them, outnumbering her, and calling her awful, profane names in front of all the neighborhood children and parents. My family did not know the extent of the harassment until Natalie told us because we barely went to church. Even on days we did go, we only attended sacrament, the first of three hours of Mormon church service.

Mat was in sixth grade at the time and reported one day that someone had carved 666 into the school locker of one of Natalie's kids. Stuff like that became routine. I guess I shouldn't have been surprised because Mat had already mentioned that the Mormon kids liked to refer to themselves as the "Mormon Mafia." They stuck to their own kind and didn't tolerate people who questioned or went against them. More than a clique, they'd become a self-righteous gang.

The wives of the church leadership, women who sided with Allure, actually came to my house and told me that I couldn't hang out with Natalie and her family anymore. The message was delivered in a very threatening way, the ringleader smirking while telling me this, like she lorded some power over me. Honestly, I didn't understand—I never thought of myself as Mormon, and no one else in my immediate family had ever been officially brought into the church in any way. To me, religion didn't play into my friendship with Natalie, so being told by someone connected with both the church and the Allure Foundation that we could no longer be friends made no logical sense.

I was not impressed. I would not abandon Natalie in what I quickly realized was her time of need. Instead, I became even more determined that our family would stand by them. That's what friends do.

And I thought that was also what good people did. I was a reluctant investigator of the church; I didn't even want to go to the Mormon church and barely attended. Even when we did go, we were always late and sat in the back. At sacrament, the only hour we occasionally attended, people walked up and talked about how great the Mormon church was. They sang songs and then handed out bread and water for communion. They used water instead of wine because Mormons don't drink alcohol. At best, we went to the church once every two to three months. We didn't attend Sunday school or any of the religious church functions; we knew nothing of the Mormons or the Book of Mormon. We still did not have a Bible in the house, and these supposed higher-up wives of the local Mormon ward's leadership had the audacity to tell me who I could and could not be friends with. It really pissed me off.

I asked these women flat out, "Are you kidding me? I'm not even Mormon. Our family are investigators of your church, and *this* is the way you behave? Holy shit." I stared them down, saying slowly and clearly, "We're investigators, and you're *threatening* me?"

They left, but they didn't quit.

Distraught, Natalie told me that these women followed her to her kids' basketball games and called her obscene names. She couldn't even go to the grocery store without being harassed. It was nonstop. Natalie would go for walks around Mission Viejo, to enjoy the natural beauty of their neighborhood, but because the harassment was so prevalent, she asked me to go with her. So then the Mormon wives followed *us*, stalked us, screamed at us. But at least I knew I was doing the right thing by my friend. Natalie wasn't alone.

I asked myself again and again if this was an accurate and acceptable depiction of Mormon behavior. Was this what we should expect of their brand of Christianity? I thought back to the woman who had ranted about Starbucks and supermarket magazines. Maybe she was a more authentic depiction of this ward's behavior than Jay and I had expected!

In the Mormon church, there's an organization called the Relief Society, which is specifically so the women of a ward learn how to be better wives, mothers, and members of the church. Not wanting Natalie to be alone in a hostile church, I bit the bullet and attended the second church hour so she had someone nearby. One day, I was walking with Natalie from a Relief Society meeting through the children's area of the church. That day, Natalie was supposed to teach Sunday school to primary school children. Two men walked up to her; both of them were well-known lawyers and powerful, influential men in the ward. There, in the middle of the hall, they started screaming and swearing at Natalie, all in front of the little kids heading to Sunday school.

I couldn't believe what I was witnessing and briefly froze in shock. These men were verbally assaulting a woman in a church and in front of children. Natalie broke down right there in the hall and fell to the floor. I grabbed her, helped her up, and urged, "Just walk away." I got her out of there, but those guys kept screaming like maniacs. The abuse did not end with the parents; Tony and Natalie's kids were equally bullied, both in and out of church by these Mormons.

Then one day after school, Tony's oldest boy called our house and told me in a strained voice, "Ali, I need your help." He was only a year older than Mat, and I could tell he was crying.

I immediately drove over to their home and discovered Natalie having what I can only describe as a nervous breakdown. Everything had just become too much. She was lying on their floor in her pajamas, bawling her head off and absolutely despondent. The children were standing all around her, sobbing. It was three o'clock in the afternoon, and her new baby was still in his jammies, and his diaper hadn't been changed.

My heart broke for all of them. Although I didn't know exactly what to do, I knew I had to do *something*, so I leaped into action, changing the baby's diaper, calling Tony, and doing my best to comfort the kids. Tony raced home and pulled Natalie up off the floor while I took all the kids to my house.

What happened to the founder of the Allure Foundation and how the whole thing was resolved was not something we cared to discover. Tony and Natalie knew they could no longer be a part of the local Mormon ward. Rather than not rocking the boat or turning a blind eye to the church's involvement in wrongdoing, Tony had made a hard choice, and it destroyed them socially. There's a concept called "sympathetic resonance" in music, and sometimes it crosses into psychology. Tony mentioned it once as one of their reasons for moving. In sympathetic resonance, when you pluck a string and another string vibrates, it creates a vibration that everything similarly tuned reacts to, adding to the richness and completeness of the sound. It's essentially the idea of a group of like-minded individuals giving off the same vibe. In Tony and Natalie's case, as beautiful as their house was, as gorgeous as the neighborhood was, they weren't in tune—they couldn't vibe—with the song that the Mission Viejo ward wanted them to sing along to. They knew they didn't fit in, so they moved away to a place they thought would be better and healthier for their whole family.

After everything that we'd seen with the Mission Viejo ward and the behavior of its members, we stopped going to that church altogether. Why be involved with people like that? I'd never witnessed anything so horrific as what the members of that ward did to Tony and Natalie's family.

They had been crucified by people claiming to be Christian.

When Bishop Jensen finally returned from caring for his daughter, I explained all about the trouble we'd been experiencing and how the whole thing left a bad taste in our mouths about actually joining the church. Really, who would want to when, if you made the right ethical choice, you were persecuted by people claiming to be your brothers and sisters in Christ?

Around that time, we learned our first request for our children to be baptized had been turned down. The church tried to make it seem like the request was rejected because we wanted Bishop Jensen to perform the ceremony, and he was no longer the ward's bishop. However, we suspected it was because we stood by Tony and Natalie and their kids instead of being bystanders or joining the ranks of their persecutors.

Bishop Jensen quietly listened to everything that had gone on in his absence and to the concerns we had about the Mission Viejo church before making a suggestion. Then Bishop Jensen—the man I'd always think of as *our* bishop—didn't make excuses for the ward, didn't promise they'd evolve and be better, but suggested instead that we leave the church. I would have been surprised except that Bishop knew us, loved us, and had never led us down the wrong path. He'd always looked out for us and earnestly wanted what was best for us. Knowing he felt our leaving was the best thing for our family to do made our decision even easier. It felt more like a relief than a rejection—Bishop wanted us safe and made it clear he felt the ward was no longer safe for our family. He even suggested we not let any more Mormons into our house—he was clearly worried for our safety.

When it became obvious that we were leaving the church, the new bishop sought us out and suggested, "Why don't you just get these kids baptized? It's just a quick dip, it's no big deal."

It was odd and made me wonder if it was somehow a numbers game. We knew the church was trying to rebrand its image and get new members; we knew the local ward had recently lost more people because of the scandal. The new bishop became really pushy about it, even though he didn't want Bishop Jensen to perform the baptism and had already turned down our baptism request once. It was like they were trying to truly reel us in, to get us to commit beyond being investigators by waving baptism before us like we were fish seeing a baited hook.

I looked at him like he was insane and then said, "Yeah, after what we just witnessed at this church!" I shrugged. "You all denied our request to have our children baptized anyway," I reminded him.

He brushed off my point about them turning us down and instead said, "I don't know why you have a problem with baptism. It's just a quick dunk in the water."

I was extremely offended. If they could treat Tony and Natalie like that, they could treat me like that too. And what made him think I wanted my kids in a church with these people? Yeah, right! I had already made the decision to leave and it felt liberating, as if a heavy weight was taken off my shoulders. Why would I ever drag my kids into that hell for a church I myself did not believe in?

"Sorry," I said, "but if that quick dip gets you into a church like this? Not interested." There was no way in hell my kids would be baptized into *that* stupid church.

# Chapter 11

AFTER OUR MISADVENTURE in the Mormon church, for four years, we focused instead on our own family. It was great; I loved every second not being connected to that place. We could spend our weekends freely; we went straight back to what made us happy in the first place. Things went back to our normal, happy life.

Although small compared to his brother Mat, Jake definitely found his place in football. He and Mat played Pop Warner football for years, Mat getting the nickname of "Mat the Merciless" for his massive size and ability to roll right across the opposition. The boys studied the plays, committing each one to memory. They started to understand strategy and began to recognize the importance of putting thought and action together to win at things they might have thought impossible. They became warriors on the football field. I never missed a game, and watching the boys play on weekends was a highlight for Jay.

Jake was tremendously fast on the football field and had this ability of tuning out everything but the game. He'd see that ball and focus so intensely nothing else existed—everything else went black. He was so good that the coach moved him around to play different positions. He was a defensive end, a fullback—you name it, he did it!

The boys became so busy with sports, and since Cydney was going to all their games and practices to support them anyhow, we got her into cheerleading. Her practices were the same days, too, and unlike the stereotypical cheerleading squad featured in movies, the cheerleaders at our kids' school weren't the popular kids. During our time in California, we realized cheerleading was totally different from how it's often portrayed, and that was a good thing. Besides, Cydney was the cutest little thing and the tiniest girl on the squad, and she had a great time cheering her brothers on, but joining cheerleading didn't make her popular. It just allowed her to be more involved and have her own sports-related fun. Everyone in the family was getting healthier through exercise and learning the value of teamwork.

When the kids weren't at school or at something sports-related, we were often hosting parties for the sports teams at our place. It was just what we did—we made friends and we had fun. Our kids didn't have bad days—they just enjoyed life.

Every weekend, something fun was happening—life without church and the ward was so much better! It was like night and day. We woke up, excited to see what new adventure each day would bring and went to bed happy each night. Motorcycling, skimboarding, trips to the amusement parks—we did it all.

Bishop Jensen still dropped by every two or three months, just to say hi, but he was much more hands-off now. Merely a friendly observer checking in. We'd chat briefly, but he knew better than to try and encourage us back into the church—it just wasn't right for us. Time passed. Jake was getting ready to hit high school, Mat was looking well into high school, and Cydney was moving along through elementary. The kids continued to grow and thrive.

Life was good, and it seemed even better without God.

In Mat's sophomore year of high school, he was challenged by his buddies to go out for rugby, so he decided to go for it—even though his friends chickened out at the last minute! Mat was the youngest player on their high school team. As he joined his first scrum, all of the boys packed tightly together, heads down, arms and legs interwoven with hands on each other's thighs, in something that from the outside almost looks like a huddle. One of the boys—a big, blond-haired, blue-eyed South African kid—looked at Mat and said, "Hey, new kid, remember to grab the shorts, not the balls!" They all roared with laughter and charged into the game.

They were a rough-and-tumble group—they had to be in order to advance in a sport as brutal as rugby. It seemed like every game, someone had something cut or broken. One kid broke his nose and, blood still dripping, went right back out to play. Another kid had his ear torn. Did it stop him from playing? No. The big South African kid's dad would shout reminders to the boys to keep their heads down. We'd all hope for the best, and they'd charge down the field like battle-hardened warriors.

I asked Mat if he didn't want to reconsider, but he was having a great time and enjoyed the camaraderie and the challenge of it all.

As a mom, after I realized how rough the sport was, I was horrified to know that my eldest son was playing something so much like football but without pads. My worry that Mat would get hurt like so many other boys kept me as close to the field as possible at all of his games and practices.

One day, they were out practicing at the park, and we all noticed the big South African kid running back and forth between the field and the bathroom with his hand covering his butt. Concerned, we asked if he was okay. Without missing a beat, he turned and looked at us, saying with a deadpan expression, "Don't eat the Indian food," and then they all laughed and got right back into practice.

That weekend, the team had a game. The opposing team was made of mostly Tongan giants. These guys were all over six feet and sported full beards and mustaches. They didn't look like they could possibly be high schoolers. They were too big, broad, and developed. I was so certain that they were older than they should have been that I boldly said to their coach, "I want to see their IDs. Those aren't children—those are men."

My request to verify their age was ignored, so I told our coach I wasn't letting Mat play against them. Mat was a child, after all, and they looked distinctly like they were full-grown men. It wouldn't have been fair or safe for my son. I made Mat sit out, and a number of other players' parents did the same with their kids. Seeing what I'd seen, Mat didn't give me any trouble about making that choice. Little did either of us know then that Mat had sat out his last rugby game.

That game was rougher than any of the others, players colliding with each other and heads knocking into one another. Afterward, everyone went home and, eventually, exhausted from playing, went to sleep. There was nothing remarkable about it until the next morning when we got word that the big blond South African kid had never woken up. He had died in his sleep.

We were all devastated. The next week, the scheduled game was postponed so everyone could attend the funeral. Mat was one of the boys asked to help carry his friend's coffin into the church. We sat there, stunned and brokenhearted, while the boy's father spoke about how he kissed his son good night every night. After everything had concluded, the boy's dad found Mat in the crowd and wrapped his arms around him. Mat lifted him up, and they hugged for a long time, both of them crushed by their surprising loss. Then he reminded Mat again, "Keep your head down," and we headed out to the car.

Once in the car, Mat said softly, "We're done. I'm not doing this anymore."

So we pulled him off the team, understanding completely that it would never again be the same for any of those boys. This was not Mat's first experience with death, and each time, it hit close to home and forced Mat to grow up a little bit faster. Rugby had more than served its purpose anyhow—Mat was always very quiet, not particularly popular, and would out read his teachers. He had a tremendous reputation with his teachers, but he had some friends at school, although he didn't have many, and he didn't always have the best. Rugby had given him more friends—and taken one away—and any bullies remaining in the neighborhood thought twice about taking him on once they realized what hard-hitting sports he was in.

During those years, I was always running in different directions, sometimes picking up one kid from elementary, then one from middle school, and one from high school. There was no time for me to work and certainly no time to give much thought to God or religion.

While cleaning up Mat's room and putting away his laundry one day, I found something strange in one of his drawers. Sometimes digging around in a fifteen-year-old's sock drawer can be dicey, but what I found in Mat's didn't alarm me as much as make me wonder. It was a Bible. Taking it gently out of his drawer, I noticed the golden stamp in the lower right corner of the book's deep-red cover reading "Placed by the Gideons." It was a Bible from the Marriott we'd stayed in on our last vacation. I was surprised and a little offended, honestly. I didn't know why he hadn't told me about it nor why he had taken it. We had money, and I would have been fine buying one for him. I found it funny, too, that, although he took the Bible, he hadn't bothered picking up the Book of Mormon, which had shared the same drawer at our hotel. Maybe it was because I'd noticed that while we had been a part of the Mission Viejo ward, the Mormon church had spent more time talking and teaching about Joseph Smith and the Book of Mormon than Jesus and the Bible to the point it sometimes felt like they had a different god.

Most people took the extra soap and shampoo out of their hotel room. Not my Mat. He'd gone straight for the meatiest book.

When he got back from school, I showed it to him and said, "I found this in your drawer while I was cleaning your room."

"Yeah."

"You know, it's okay if you want to read the Bible," I said. "I will one hundred percent support you."

"Okay," he said.

I wondered if he had sensed how anti-religion I was and that had made him shy about his curiosity.

"I just wanted to know if there's a god," he said.

"Okay." My eldest son, the avid reader, was looking for proof of God's existence between the pages of the Bible. It seemed entirely suitable.

It was a hot day on the football field, and the teams were well matched. They rewarded the kids' successes with stickers, and Jake was a powerful enough player that his helmet and shoulder pads were thick with stickers. He got stickers for smart plays, for great moves, and especially for the really big tackles. Taking down players hard was part of the game, and, like each of his teammates, Jake got a sticker each time he flattened a player.

The only problem was that Jake also had asthma. On hot, sunny, or windy days, he'd play for as long as he could, but inevitably he'd need a break and he'd come jogging off the field to get a dose of albuterol. I always carried what Jake needed for his breathing treatments and, as soon as he could, he'd go right back in.

I had become the team's photographer, which allowed me to be all over, taking action shots of the kids. More importantly, though, it allowed me to be close to Jake so that when he got tired or started feeling tightness in his chest, he could let me know. They played him so often and so hard—and he was so vital to their success—that he wouldn't always tell them when he needed a minute for a breathing treatment. But I was there, he'd tell me. He loved the rush of the game; he loved the action.

It was easy to see how alive he felt playing football. On and off the field taking photographs, I kept a close eye on Jake. Days like this were especially brutal on his asthma. The breathing treatments were frequent and vital, and the pressure to beat the opposing team was high. The coaches pulled Jake aside after he'd completed another dose of albuterol, and rather than asking how my son was doing or worrying over him, they looked at him and ordered, "Take out the QB." Given his marching orders, he took his position, focused on the other team's quarterback, and slammed into him. Their position on the field shifted and Jake rammed him again. Finally, once more face-to-face, the quarterback said, "Stay away," but Jake flattened him with such force that the kid's shoes were blown straight off. Back on the sideline, the coaches roared with laughter at Jake's success.

Our team was victorious. Jake was a beast.

It was then I really realized what was happening. It was one thing to be a warrior on the football field, to throw your heart into something and fight until you won, but it was another to be manipulated into brutal behavior by men standing on the sidelines. I walked over to the coaches and said, "Don't use my kid to take people out. Use your own kid if you want to do that."

As brutal as Jake was on the football field, he knew how to separate football from the rest of his life. He hung out with the underdogs as much as he hung out with anyone else—just like we did. None of us cared if you had money or if you were popular. What mattered more was the sort of person you were. Neither Mat nor Jake were typical jocks—they were good kids, even if they were absolute beasts on the football field.

One Saturday morning, fog rolling in from the ocean carried a damp chill that laid a layer of tiny droplets on everything. The football field was lit with sun, but there was an eeriness to the atmosphere because of the lingering mist that seemed to ring the field.

Coach stepped out onto the turf, licked his finger, and held it up to test the air. He looked at the other coach and then at us and announced with a grin, "This is Jake weather." The humidity was perfect for an asthmatic like Jake.

Jake was so intense that the coaches loved him, and the opposing teams feared him. He played so fiercely that coaches sometimes suggested if he wasn't taken out of the game they'd wind up with half their team hurt. Inevitably, the other team would quickly identify Jake as a threat and do whatever they could to stop or slow him down. That game, one kid grabbed him by his jersey and held on tight, trying to keep Jake from making any progress. Annoyed when the kid would not let go, Jake grabbed his face mask and kneed him right in the balls. Back on the sidelines, Jake was greeted by the coaches with a fist bump.

As a defensive end, Jake loved hurling his entire body into an opponent to knock them off their feet. He'd nearly go into a trance on the football field, catching sight of the ball and letting the rest of the world drop away in darkness. The next thing Jake knew, he was on top of his target! I watched from the sidelines as Jake jumped up, his cleated foot on his opposition's chest, and roared like a wild animal having just made a kill.

In the stands and on the sidelines, everyone went nuts—absolutely thrilled! But amid the yelling and Gatorade-dumping of the celebration, I couldn't help but wonder if my son Jake was becoming more beast than boy. As a mom, did I need to do something to change his attitude? I wanted him to be strong, but was this too much? Boys don't come with instruction manuals, so I decided to give it some thought.

# Chapter 12

THE NEXT DAY something deep inside Jake shifted. He grew quiet, introspective, and reclusive. His behavior seemed night-and-day. And then, just a few days after the football game where he'd been a conqueror, he came to me crying, just a boy—a boy talking about seeing God. I did everything I could as a mother. I was stunned, but I listened. I was gentle and supportive and absolutely awestruck and full of questions. My first instinct was always to reach out to my husband and Jay offered what help he could, but it boiled down to suggesting I dig up Bishop Jensen's business card. So I did. We were desperate.

On the other end of the phone, Bishop Jensen had fallen silent, taking it all in. "And this was Jake, you said? Not Mat?"

"It was definitely Jake," I replied, wondering if maybe I shouldn't have called. How would anyone listening to me not think that my son was crazy? And that I was crazy, too, for believing him?

Not only had I interrupted Bishop Jensen at work at his law firm, but I was asking him to believe some pretty wild stuff and to help us deal with it.

As astonished as Bishop Jensen was about what I was saying, and which of my children had told me all of it, he'd gotten to know our family pretty well over the past few years. He'd become like a grandfather figure to them, gradually filling a void in our family. Bishop knew Mat as the family's strong, studious, independent member. He knew Cydney was the sweet artistic butterfly. And Bishop Jensen also understood that Jake was the rambunctious couldn't-keep-still kid—the liveliest of the lot.

But, suddenly, here we were, and Jake had spoken to God.

"Ali," Bishop Jensen said, "listen. I need to ask you some questions."

"Okay."

"Has Jake seen any frightening or disturbing movies recently?"

*Not unless you consider Waterboy disturbing*, I thought about it. With school and Pop Warner football practice, the boys were on a very regimented schedule. "I mean, he's seen *Goonies*. But mostly he still watches kids' shows. *Scooby-Doo*, *SpongeBob SquarePants*, stuff like that."

"Was he playing any video games prior to this?" Bishop asked.

"No, not really. Not anything like this, all he played was *Call of Duty*." When Jake did have time after school, football, and homework, he played some games, but mostly, he watched the Discovery Channel. He thought Steve Irwin was the coolest guy ever and enjoyed reruns of *The Crocodile Hunter*.

"Has he read any scary or weird books?" Bishop Jensen tried.

"No," I assured him, because as smart as my kids were, Jake wasn't big on reading any sort of book at the time.

"Did Jake see or do anything that he might have been exposed to that could have provoked an experience like this?" My brain was going in so many different directions I barely realized he was quiet until he spoke again. "I'm going to pray about this, Ali, and when I get done at work, I'll give you a call."

What could I say? That I was desperate? That I needed more help and sooner? "Okay, Bishop, but...Jake's crying a lot," I confessed.

There was briefly silence on the line. "I'll pray and I'll call," Bishop assured me. "But I need you to do a couple things at least until I call you back, okay?"

"Yes, Bishop," I said, feeling embarrassed and trying to play it cool.

"Don't let Jake go anywhere alone. Don't let him out of your sight, you understand?"

"Yes."

"And Ali?"

"Yes, Bishop?"

"Don't talk to anyone else about any of this. Not yet."

"Not a problem," I said.

"I'm going to go now and pray," he said. "I'll call you after work. Take care, Ali."

"You too, Bishop."

I sat back down with the kids. "Bishop's going to say a prayer, and he'll call back after work," I explained. I glanced at the clock. It was just after three. If Bishop Jensen was planning on keeping regular business hours, we were going to have a while to wait.

As strange as it was, I *did* believe Jake. He wasn't the sort of kid who could string together such an elaborate and specific story. His ADHD made it hard for him to even pay the level of attention needed to construct such a complicated story out of thin air.

We'd tried putting him on the suggested medications to help him with his ADHD, but they made him feel sluggish and depressed, so we'd returned to my stand-by of Excedrin and Coca-Cola. It helped take the edge off, but the amount of intense focus and creativity Jake would have needed to make something like this up? It simply wasn't in him. I had to believe my son had seen something—and something incredible—because nothing else made sense. It was too phenomenal not to have happened. He was never this emotional. He was a tough kid, not someone who cried. This wasn't like him.

"We all believe you," I said, reaching out to my youngest boy.

"Yeah," Mat said, "this is Jake we're talking about. He's never so much as picked up a Bible, let alone learned anything about God or his throne room."

I agreed. Jake wasn't the sort to even think about God; it was like pulling teeth just to get Jake to sit down long enough to pick up a book. His curiosity didn't include God. Football games, yes. Girls, sure. But God had never been one of his interests.

Together, we focused on trying to cheer Jake up, but he was miserable, and this wasn't like the normal Mom stuff I had prepared for. Bad grades, broken bones, even broken hearts, sure. But this?

This was beyond anything I'd considered needing to understand as someone's mother.

The phone rang and I was surprised to find Bishop on the other end. He'd called back much sooner than I'd expected. "Ali," he said, "I need you guys to stay next to Jake. I don't want anyone to leave him alone. You have Mat and Cydney stay right by him and don't let him leave that room."

"Okay."

"I prayed about it," he explained, "and I saw everything. I'll be right there." And then, without another word, he hung up the phone. Honestly, him suddenly hanging up the phone was just one more in a list of things that freaked me out that day. Bishop wasn't known for just hanging up on someone. But then, too, Jake wasn't known for having chats with God.

About fifteen minutes later, I answered a knock at our door and found Bishop Jensen standing there, just as calm and sweet as usual. "Where is Jake?"

Speechless, I stepped aside to let him past and closed the door, following him as he made a beeline to the kids, still curled up together on the couch.

Mormon bishops are trained to answer the many needs of the people in their wards, and Bishop Jensen took his responsibility seriously. He came into our home and immediately sat down with the group of us, positioning himself on the cushioned coffee table, directly across from Jake, and took his hands in his own. "Jake, tell me what you saw."

Gulping down a ragged breath, Jake again rolled out the details of his vision in exactly the same words and way he'd told me, only halting to get a tissue and try again to pull himself together. He sobbed and shook, but he got the words out. When he had finally finished reliving his meeting with God and the horrible battle that followed, he whispered, "Where was my daddy?" Jake cried even harder. "I didn't see him."

"Don't worry about your dad," Bishop soothed. He patted Jake on the leg and sat back. "God will take care of your dad."

Bishop looked at Mat and Cydney and ordered, "You stay by your brother. Don't leave this room. Mat, take care of your little brother." Then he looked at me. "Ali, would you come with me, please?"

"Of course."

Bishop took me outside. The sun shone bright above in the clear blue sky, and the air smelled sweet. For most Californians, it was just another gorgeous day. Bishop reached out and rested his hand on my shoulder. "Ali, right when we hung up, I knelt down, and I said a prayer. I asked God for guidance, and in my prayer, I saw the entire vision. Everything Jake just said in there? I saw it too," he reported, and I saw tears in his eyes.

I nearly doubled over releasing a sigh of relief. He didn't think we were crazy. He believed Jake too. He had even seen it all for himself! "That's such a relie—"

But before I could even finish the word, Bishop continued, "But here's the thing I need you to understand. It's not over. God didn't show him everything. There's more to come. God's going to keep visiting Jake. Your goal needs to be to keep Jake sane."

Any sense of relief I'd felt was sucked right away. Suddenly, the sun didn't seem as bright, and there was a chill in the air. I wasn't sure I wanted to hear any more. I wasn't ready. Not for something like this.

"For God to choose a boy of this age," Bishop said, "is unheard of. You'll always have to watch him, always protect him because sometimes, when you see these sorts of things, it's too much." He got quiet then, letting it sink in. "It's too much for people to see these things, Ali. God's too big, you understand? He's too much for the human soul or body. So Jake needs to be protected from this point forward. God's not done with him. There's more to come."

I had no words. My son was already so badly wounded. He was sobbing in our family room. To entertain the idea that this wasn't over? That it wasn't a one-off? That it was just the start? It was a lot to take in.

"Jake's been chosen by the Lord," Bishop said. "I believe that."

I was stunned. There I was, a woman who struggled with religion—who was, in many ways, a newcomer to it—and this man who I trusted and who had been religious all his life was telling me all our lives were going to be forever changed because God had chosen my son. It seemed so strange and so absolutely unfair. Jake hadn't asked for this—none of us had.

For a moment, I wasn't sure I could keep breathing. My mind rebelled. No book I'd ever read, no conversation I'd had with friends who had kids the same age—nothing had prepared me for this. There was no *Dr. Phil* episode, no advice from *Oprah* that would help with this situation. And Jay… My sweet, wonderful husband was even more out of touch with God than I was. I felt so alone, so ill-equipped to do whatever it was that Jake would need now.

"Ali?" Bishop's calm voice broke through my panic. I realized his hand was still on my shoulder, a steadying and grounding weight. He had to know more about these sorts of things than I did. He had been a religious man all his life.

I somehow caught my breath and decided to roll with the punches because I had no other choice. "Okay," I said with a gulp.

"Listen," Bishop said, "you'll need to change your lives and learn how to pray, Ali. In order to protect your family, you'll need to pay close attention to everything I do inside this house. I'll come back from time to time, to check in and help out. But there will be times when you have to do some of the cleaning I'll do today but without me. Do you understand?"

"Sure." I didn't understand. I didn't have a clue what he was talking about, but I knew I needed to pay close attention to everything he did next so I could do it too. Not an easy feat for a worried mom with her own ADHD.

Bishop and I returned to the kids, and he laid his hands on each of us in turn, blessing us and asking that God protect us. Bible in hand, he asked me, "Do you have that calendar I gave you?"

"Yes." I knew the calendar he meant. He had given us one for Christmas, featuring a different image of Jesus Christ each month. It wasn't something I'd normally hang in my house—it didn't go with our family's style—so, although I'd accepted it graciously, I had tucked it away in a box. "Let me get it," I said. "I'll be right back!"

"And tape," Bishop called after me. "I'll also need Scotch tape."

When I returned, he began cleaning the house with prayer. Together, he and I walked into each room, and I watched as Bishop tore a picture of Christ free from the calendar and taped it above each door, praying the whole time. By the time he was finished, there was an image of Jesus above every door in the house: bedroom, bathroom, living room, kitchen. Suddenly, Jesus was visibly present in each.

Leaving the kids together in the family room, Bishop and I ventured to Jake's room. I paused at the threshold. There was a cold that seeped out of my son's room and went straight into my bones, the sort of cold that sticks and never seems quite right in a place like sunny California. Standing there, feeling just a brush with that cold air, I got an even clearer understanding of what Jake had felt, seeing and hearing all those awful things while God taught him how to tell the difference between messages—and messengers—of both the good and evil. There, in my youngest son's room, Bishop Jensen got down on his knees and prayed fervently on our behalf, and I waited with him, stunned to see someone doing what he was, and praying that his prayers would work.

By the time all was said and done, Bishop had blessed everything. And I mean everything! The pipes, air vents, windows, air conditioner, heater, the attic. Any path in or out of our house received Bishop's blessing and his request that sentinels protect our house.

Eventually, when Bishop felt he had finished, I walked him to the door and thanked him. I wasn't sure how much his blessings and prayers could really do, but there was already a fresh sense of comfort in the house, and I was willing to try anything. "Ali," he said, "I need you to remember everything I said to you today, including not saying anything about this to anybody else. Your work's just beginning. Your family needs to pray every morning and constantly, if you can. You all need to read your Scriptures, and, most importantly, all of you need to keep the Lord close. In your heart, in your mind, in your soul. You must do everything you can to protect Jake and keep your lives as peaceful as possible. You need to keep a tight ship. Keeping that peace and calm can help keep evil away. I want you to also consider getting the children baptized."

"Oh," I said, thinking about my own experience with baptism and how little I knew about it. "I'm not sure about that."

He stepped outside and turned back around to look at me as I stood there in the doorway of my family's beautiful house built in such a good neighborhood, a safe neighborhood. I was just a mom, ready to do anything to protect my kids—if only I had the right weapons. "Try thinking of it as giving you additional fighting power," he said. "In the battle for a person's soul, baptism is your shield."

I still wasn't completely sold on it. I thought we'd been doing pretty well the way we'd been going, until this strange hiccup happened. But this was just a weird fluke. Even if this wasn't a once-and-done thing, how long could it possibly go on?

Baptism, though, seemed like such a permanent solution to what was surely only a temporary problem. I wanted to make sure the kids could choose their faith and were ready to commit to their choice, but only when they were sure and ready. I didn't want them to feel forced into baptism and certainly not in any way that was like I had been. But maybe baptism didn't mean you were stuck being Mormon. Maybe that was more a matter of the effect of the commitment someone made.

"See, Ali, when God or angels come to people," he explained, "or when you're chosen by the Lord to do some sort of work, evil also knows you're chosen. And if there's one thing evil wants, it's to thwart the Lord and his people's good works. Jake's been chosen. I have no doubt. And because you're his mom, you've been chosen to protect him. Evil will try to stop you. Each one of you," he warned. "Your family needs to get to a level of reverence with the Lord, Christ, and the Holy Spirit, so that when evil comes, you can handle it. Because it will come, Ali. It's only a matter of time."

## Chapter 13

*2009*

KEEPING BISHOP JENSEN'S words of warning in mind, we followed his advice. We prayed a lot and we read a lot of Scripture. We found some comfort in searching for answers and trying to understand what Jake had seen and what it might have meant for our family.

Football became more of a chore than a passion for both of the boys. They went from being powerhouse jocks to reading as much as they could. We were all trying desperately to figure out what the things Jake had seen actually meant. One day, after football practice, Jake actually said to me, "I'm glad God came to me in a vision. I was about to tell you I didn't believe in him."

As ready as Jake had been to give up on God, clearly God hadn't been ready for Jake to give up on *him*, and as much as Jake was hurting, he was still grateful. To me, it seemed Jake had never had a bad day in his life, and then God came along, and everything got turned upside down. Our house became very active. Unexplained stuff became commonplace. It was as if Jake's vision had stirred something up in the house or drawn something to it.

We devoured every book in the Bible; we marked and highlighted any passage we thought was important. We found things in the Bible and other resources that seemed right out of Jake's vision, and those things gave us comfort. Mat had a gift for research, and he'd find things and share them. "Part of Jake's vision is like it says in the Bible," Mat said one day, "in Revelation 4:6. John talks about a sea of glass, like crystal in God's throne room.

"The twenty-four elders, your description of God, the golden throne, the lions, the crystal floor, God's pedestal being the Earth," Mat stated, "these things tell me you saw something." Mat left us briefly and returned with his Marriott Bible. He quickly opened it to the chapter that talked about God's throne room. "What Jake saw is right here, written in Revelations," he justified, looking from me to Cydney before looking back to Jake.

Too soon, more odd things started happening. We would hear weird noises the house didn't normally make: tapping on the walls and doors, random banging, the sound of the scratching of nails along the wall, muffled voices, guttural growls, or the sound of unexplained footsteps at night. Jake would occasionally try to catch glimpses out the door when he heard a noise. Sometimes a dark-hooded shadow figure would walk in his room. As soon as it happened, he would come straight to me, and I'd immediately check it out.

I never saw the hooded figure, but I cleaned each room with prayer in the name of God, Jesus, and the Holy Spirit, no matter how terrified I was, no matter how much my body or my voice shook with fear.

Often we would hear a muffled voice call our names. I'd be doing something in one room and would hear my name called by Jake, Mat, or Cydney. Or so I thought. But none of the kids had actually called for me or were in a part of the house where I would have heard them call. I'd hear them call my name when none of them were even home, every single time the voice a perfect mimic of one of the kids. The same thing happened to each one of my kids. Something was watching us, keeping to the dark places of the house, and it knew each of our names and could perfectly imitate our voices. I would sometimes find myself afraid to enter one of our house's many rooms, every instinct in my body telling me to run away, the hairs on my arms standing up straight, my heart pounding out of my chest. It was terrifying, and every time, I walked into the room where the unexplained noises originated, my stomach twisted and turned, and I became physically sick.

One evening after school, packing the next day's lunches for the kids, I was downstairs helping Cydney with her bath, the bathroom door open so I could keep an eye—and an ear—out. Cydney suddenly said, "Mom, there's a man standing out there."

"There is nothing there." I looked out the door into the hall and saw nothing.

"Mom, there's somebody out there," Cydney insisted.

I looked again, peering out the bathroom door, into the dark hall, even out the glass double doors that led into our private courtyard and provided a hint of light. Nothing. I was frazzled. It was bad enough feeling alone some weeks and raising three kids, but heaping all the weirdness on top of it?

Cydney was adamant, insisting again and again that someone lurked in the hall outside.

"Fine, I'll go look," I said, striding out of the brightly lit bathroom and into the much dimmer hallway. I drew up short, seeing a hulking black figure toward the hall's end. "Holy shit!"

Standing there, facing down the shadowy figure, the sound of Cydney's worries in my ears, I felt the shadow figure's intentions. In my mind's eye, I saw Jake bathing in a tub, something he never did, and a long spindly arm reached toward him, and a mummified-looking hand pressing Jake's head under the water and holding him under.

I knew then what the shadow wanted and why it was here.

I ran back into the bathroom, plucked Cydney out of the water, bubbles still in her hair, wrapped her in a towel, and raced up the stairs with my dripping daughter. Jake's bathroom door was locked. I always respected the privacy of my kids, but at this moment, I needed to get Jake out of the water. Holding Cydney, I pounded on the door and fought with the knob, shouting, "Jake, are you okay? Get out of the tub!"

Somehow, I got through the first door, but the second door was also locked. Mat came running in from his room, and I handed Cydney to him, still yelling, "Get out of the tub!" as Jake, still in the tub, reached over and opened the door. I pulled him out of the tub, threw a towel to him, and escorted him down the dark hall and to my room. Mat, still toting Cydney, followed.

I shut my door and turned to Jake. My heart thumping, I struggled for words, scared. I felt like I'd been moments away from losing my youngest boy. "Jake, are you okay? Did you see anything? Feel anything?"

He said he hadn't.

I explained to him what I saw and about this thing's desire to drown him. I told him, "You've got to tell us when you are going to bathe and don't lock the door." I tossed some fresh laundry at him. With three kids in the house, there were always clean clothes in my room either waiting to be folded or ready to be put in drawers. I walked Cydney into my bathroom, rinsed the rest of the soap out of her hair, and got her dressed too.

As many things as I'd already experienced, and as many things as my children were experiencing with me, deep down, in my core, I didn't want any of it to be real. Living in a world of shadowy and dangerous figures was unsettling at best. There was no place I could go to get comprehensive how-to or DIY help, no 1800 number, no *What to Expect When* book.

I wanted only tangible, understandable things in my life. All I wanted was to be a good mom and to live out the rest of my life happily. I never wanted anything to do with the supernatural.

But something much bigger than me had other plans.

One particular night, we heard long fingernails scratching along the walls of the stairs leading to Jake's bedroom. The sound was very similar to nails on a chalkboard, except deeper and louder. It ended with a knock, and Jake's door shook. Jake said this had been happening every night for weeks. He thought we were playing a trick on him and asked us to stop. But one night, Mat said he heard the same thing when Jake and he were playing video games in Jake's room with the door shut so as to not wake up the family. Mat said he heard nails drag along the wall, followed by a *knock, knock* and *tap, tap* of fingernails on the door. Then the door shook as if someone leaned against it. Having heard enough, we decided to try and catch whatever it was in action.

"Jake," I whispered, "go into your bedroom and shut the door and sit there, facing your computer like you're playing." I went back to my bedroom and waited, hiding behind my door so I could hear everything and whip around into the hallway to see who or what was causing whatever I might hear. I wanted answers.

We all sat in our positions very quietly, patiently. Within seconds, the scratching noise began midway up the stairs to Jake's room. I peeked, as fast as I could, around the corner but saw nothing. Right then, the *tap, tap, tap* started. Then the door visibly shook, ending in a big thud.

Mat whipped out of his room, saying, "I heard that!"

I'd heard it too. All three of us had heard the scratching and banging and all at the same time too. We found the undeniable proof we were looking for and we knew that whatever we had just witnessed was not good. We also had a sickly turning of our stomachs, a sense of nausea, uneasiness, a brush of cold, and a racing heart warning whenever something unexplained was about to happen. As eerie as it was, at least by discovering we all heard the same thing at the same time, we were reminded that we weren't alone in our experiences.

The activity increased to such a level that I drove out to Target and picked up a baby monitor. Without telling Jake, I put it in his room in case something happened and he needed me. With Cydney staying in my room and most of the activity seeming to center around Jake, it seemed like the most logical course of action. Knowing that if something happened, I'd hear it and be able to react helped me feel a little better about things.

Until I started hearing other noises in Jake's room.

The first night, the baby monitor was in Jake's room, we heard a noise that sounded like the flapping of wings, like a bird with its wings beating rapidly, fluttering. I imagined it was a large bug of some sort flying close to the monitor and then flitting further away but remaining near enough to be heard. I went to Jake's room and saw nothing out of the ordinary. The noise stopped until I'd returned to my own room for a while. Then it came back. I'd change the station on the monitor and adjust its location, thinking it was a signal issue. But every time—every single night—the fluttering returned.

I'd hear it, go look, see nothing, and it would cease for about thirty minutes. Then it would start up again. The noise was always at night and always when Jake was by himself and asleep. And whenever one of us walked in to try and catch whatever it was in action, the sound of fluttering would stop.

Jake, of course, slept right through all of it. He thought we were crazy when we talked later about what we were hearing, and he was surprised when I confessed I'd sneaked the baby monitor into his room to listen in on him at night.

One weekend, when Jay came home, he heard it, too, the sound of fluttering going all night long, only stopping briefly when Jake woke up because of someone checking in on him. We decided to try and recreate it. We tried the fan. On. Off. We tried the air conditioner. On. Off. Nothing made the same sound. The strange wingbeats had already gone on for months, and we had no answers. Could it be a technical issue with the monitor itself? I returned to Target and bought a second baby monitor, their best and, of course, most expensive one.

Two hundred and fifty dollars later, and it didn't make a bit of difference. The fluttering just went right on, making it nearly impossible for any of us—except Jake—to sleep. We would walk into his room and see nothing; like the fluttering, it would disappear from the baby monitor and then start up again like clockwork, shortly after we left.

Watching over Jake wore on all of us. We were all so desperate to get a good night's sleep that we brought out the air mattresses and asked everyone to move back into the master bedroom. Jake was determined to stay in his room—he wasn't hearing any fluttering. He was such a deep sleeper he didn't even notice us walking into his room at night.

That night, around midnight, Mat, Cydney, and I were still up. We were trying to figure out what the heck to do about the fluttering, and Mat said, "Stay here, Mom. Let me go this time and take a look."

Maybe his eyes would see something I was missing. "Okay."

He was gone for such a long time that I got worried. I couldn't hear Mat on the monitor. Jake's room was dead quiet except for the fluttering. I told Cydney to stay put, and I walked down the hall toward Jake's room. The first thing I noticed was the cold and then Mat standing by his door, peeking into the room.

I stepped over to him and asked, "Are you okay?"

Mat whispered, "Do you see it?"

Gradually, I made out the outline of a pale gray-hooded figure above Jake as he slept.

"Holy shit."

Mat commanded it to leave in the name of God, Jesus, and the Holy Spirit, and it disappeared as quickly as it had come. Jake, having awakened due to the noise and commotion in his room, was convinced to set up a bed in the master bedroom. Certain that we knew the source of the fluttering, I moved all the kids into my bedroom, figuring the old adage "safety in numbers" had to be worth something. We shut and locked the door. We had no real understanding of what we were dealing with.

# Chapter 14

THE NEXT NIGHT, we were just hoping to get a good night's sleep. While everyone prepared to sleep in the master bedroom, we heard the familiar fluttering, and then heavy footsteps walked from Jake's room toward us.

There was a *bang, bang, bang* on the door as if someone was knocking to come in. The door was locked, but its handle started to wiggle like there was someone on the other side, trying to come in. An empty clothes hanger hung on the doorknob, and we all watched, transfixed, as the hanger moved back and forth. Shivering, Jake, Cydney, and I huddled closer on the chairs, shocked, staring at the hanger as it followed the movement of the door handle, swinging side to side. I looked for my home phone, and beside it stood my glass on the nearby nightstand; not a ripple marked the water's surface. No tremble shook the floor or the chair. The overhead light didn't budge, not a bit. This was no earthquake.

The hanger still twisted slowly on the doorknob, turning back and forth, mesmerizing and horrifying all at once. From the queasy feeling in the pit of my stomach, I knew that whatever was out there couldn't be good. Cydney ran into the closet to hide.

Even though I had been a witness to all the supernatural happenings occurring in the house, what I was seeing and hearing made me think there was a burglar on the other side of the door. The rest of us stayed on the chairs, our heads close together, trying to figure out what to do next.

I glanced around the room, assessing my options for self-defense, and my gaze fell on the Bible and a flathead screwdriver. The Bible was pretty hefty but would be of little help against an intruder. I grabbed them both.

Gripping the phone, I dialed Jay. He had just picked up and heard my urgent whisper when suddenly, Mat—just seventeen years old—darted straight for the door. Swinging it open, he went straight into the darkness to confront whatever was out there. The breath died in my throat. My heart jumped and pounded painfully against my ribs. For one awful moment, I was frozen there, staring at the grim, black mouth of a doorway and the dark hallway into which my eldest boy had disappeared. Then, with a gulp of air, I threw the phone at Jake and ordered, "Don't leave. Stay on the phone with your dad!"

As scared as I was, I was determined my boy would not face that—whatever or whoever it might be—all alone.

I darted out the door, slamming it shut behind me. It was black as night in the hallway, with only the faint glow of the track lighting bordering the stairway, hinting at anything's shape. I was so intent on getting to Mat before something bad happened that I nearly plowed right into him. He was kneeling not far from the head of the steps. I'd learned enough by that point, that when one of my kids was praying, I fell to my knees and prayed too.

It was a simple prayer: "In the name of the Father and the Son and the Holy Spirit, we command all evil things to leave now." We hadn't been taught many specifics as far as what to say—we just went with our gut and, most importantly, with God.

Mat explained, "When I opened that door, there was a huge hooded figure—taller and wider than me—with a light gray hooded cloak wrapped around it from head to shoulder. I couldn't see its face. The hood obscured it. It was transparent, and I could see through it. I was praying to keep it at bay when you joined me. It's gone now." He stood and put a hand out to help me up.

At six-four, for Mat to say something spooky was bigger than him definitely created a disturbing image in my head. The prayer worked.

Back in my bedroom, Cydney emerged from the closet and asked why I'd interrupted her prayers. "What do you mean?" I asked.

"When I was in the closet," she said, exasperated, "I started praying there, in the quiet, and I heard someone walk in. The hangers moved like someone brushed by them. I opened up my eyes, just to take a peek, and I saw your legs."

Mat and I exchanged a worried glance.

"Well, I saw what I could of you, just you from your knees down. You were wearing your sweats and your socks. Like you are right now." She pointed at me as if to confirm what she'd seen. "It was weird, but I just continued saying my prayers. Then you walked out. I wrapped up my prayers, and here we are."

"I don't want to freak you out, sweetheart," I began, "but it wasn't me. I wasn't even in the closet, not at all."

Cydney paused and thought about it. "Oh," she said, and I knew she realized what I knew—what we all knew based on everyone's expressions—that something had made it inside the room where we thought we were the safest. After we all gathered, we walked the entire house together. We turned on all the lights, checked every bedroom, bathroom, and closet. We checked every outside door and window. They were all locked. We looked at the alarm system. It was still armed. It had not gone off. We stayed together, sharing the same space, never letting Jake out of our sight for the next couple months.

Eventually, we began to manage the unusual activity in our lives. The boys returned to their bedrooms because they were getting sick and tired of sleeping on the floor, but Cydney, a wisp of a girl, stayed with me. During the daytime, I pushed hard for all of us to live a normal life. It was an uphill battle but, I believed, one of the most important battles of my life. As much as dark and dangerous things wanted to pull our focus toward them, I wanted our family to have a full and normal life. Well, as normal as we could with the family being seemingly haunted. Most days, it was almost possible—at least in broad daylight—to believe things could be normal. The kids headed off to school, I did the things around the house I needed to, got the kids to their sports' practices: football for Jake and Mat and cheerleading for Cydney. I'd shoot photos of the kids at their practices and games and chat with other parents. There were days when things almost felt okay. But even on the good days, too often, our home life was a different story.

About a month later, I was woken by a stern voice saying clearly, "Mat needs your help." I ignored it a few times, but the voice became louder and more aggressive. Rolling over, I turned on the little light on my nightstand. Beside me, Cydney still slept peacefully, her blonde hair like a golden halo on her pillow. She looked so innocent and small. I hated leaving her, but knew I had to. Quietly, I slipped out of the bed and walked down the hall to first check on Jake, and then I walked into Mat's room.

I found Mat sitting up in his bed with the lights on. It must have been four in the morning. I asked, "What are you doing up?"

"I was sleeping and had a strange feeling that I had to go into Jake's room."

I asked, "What happened?"

Mat said, "I walked toward Jake's room, and I felt this powerful presence, but in my gut, something didn't feel right. The moment I realized something was wrong, I felt this extremely heavy weight pressing down on me as if it was trying to get me to kneel. A large, black-hooded figure, much taller than I am, appeared in the corner of the room. My head began to spin, and it made me want to fall to my knees. I gathered every bit of my strength to remain standing and forced myself to walk over to the corner and pray. When I couldn't handle the weight anymore, I decided to kneel and continue praying to God for what felt like hours. I prayed until, eventually, the heavy weight began to lighten, and I continued to pray until the weight and uneasiness went away. The hooded figure disappeared, and I finally got up, off my knees."

I looked down at Mat's knees. They were bruised from the extended time he spent on them, praying in Jake's room.

Mat continued, "I walked back into my room and sat on my bed. The mirrored closet doors in front of me faded away, and the entire room turned gray and expanded outward. Then thousands upon thousands of deformed and twisted beings with weapons, their numbers going as far back as I could see, appeared out of nowhere."

Mat had gathered his strength once more and prayed in the name of God, Jesus, and the Holy Spirit, and this time, everything disappeared quickly without much difficulty. "And then," he concluded, "you walked in."

I asked, "How long have you been doing this?"

He sighed and said, "A long time."

He'd known from day one that Jake needed some sort of special support, and Mat was determined to provide whatever support he could. I realized then that the tiredness I'd started to recognize in Mat, the darkening areas under his eyes that had begun to make me wonder if he was physically okay, were signs of a hard-fought exhaustion. I learned he had been watching over and protecting Jake in secret, every single night since Jake's vision.

I was mad, not at Mat but at myself and at whatever evil thing was taxing my family like this. "Why didn't you get me, Mat?" I said softly.

He shook his head and sighed, saying, "Mom. You weren't ready."

It was like a stab right to my heart. My eyes began to tear up.

"You weren't ready *with God*," he explained.

He was right. I understood the words Mat was saying; I had to stop running away from God. All those years, I hadn't had any real connection with God other than a fleeting moment here or there. Whatever bond I'd had, it hadn't been consistent nor particularly strong. Even though I believed in Jake's vision, and I witnessed unexplained happenings in the house, I still ignored the voice telling me Mat needed my help. Everything became more real, and I knew I had to take God more seriously.

Mat, even as tired as he was, saw how emotionally torn up I was and reassured, "But you are now. You're ready now, Mom," he insisted. "Which is great," he muttered, "because I'm tired." He slid under the covers of his bed and, closing his eyes, said, "Now it's your turn."

So, at least for a while, I took over watching Jake at night.

After Jake's vision, life for us changed forever. Everything went completely chaotic. In some ways, our lives felt like they were ending, but that vision was really just the beginning of a new chapter. We tried to find and maintain some sense of normalcy after Jake met God, but life was flipped on its head. Everything was so different; even the things Jake once loved and excelled at no longer held his interest. The vibrant, fun-loving Jake I'd chased after as an adventurous toddler, the little boy willing to take a swing at a grown man in a boxing ring, the teen who eagerly flung himself headfirst into a line of football players—that boy was gone. What remained of him had changed. It was as if meeting God had made him somehow feel out of place, like he didn't belong. It broke my heart.

Because of Jake's intense reputation on the football field, when the teams faced off, kids on the other side would see him and say, "Don't hurt me." Before the vision, Jake would have still crushed them and thought little of it—it was all part of the game, after all. But after the vision, he started seeing things differently. He didn't want to hurt anyone in any way. He started having conflicts with his coaches. He no longer wanted to blindly demolish other kids, just for the sake of some game.

There wasn't any fun in it anymore. He nearly quit midseason, but the team needed him, and he wanted to honor his commitment. So he played on. Late in the season, when he'd finally had enough, he told me so, and I let the coaches know we were done. I supported him 100 percent, even though Jay was disappointed because Jake was so bloody good. Jay was going to miss the games, but we had no choice but to support our kids. It was what good parents did, and our kid needed a lot of support at the time.

When Jake left football behind, it signaled an end not only to the practices, photos, and weekly games but also to the parties we frequently threw for the team. Mat left football when Jake did—by then, Mat had already quit rugby. Cydney's commitment to cheerleading wasn't very serious, and the other girls in her squad only cheered sporadically, so she stopped cheering. Our kids' involvement in sports had been the most definite sense of normalcy we had after the vision, and now it was gone too.

With no sports to steal his time and a fierce determination to help, Mat focused on trying to find answers for what was going on with his younger brother. He dove into every book on the subject he could find, reading forty or more pages of the Bible each night, while also digging into the Apocryphal books and other resources.

We believed Jake had experienced something awesome, but we wanted to understand what Jake had seen and better grasp what it all meant. We scoured the Internet for information and book suggestions and watched television shows we thought might give us some insight, including series and specials on the History Channel and *Ancient Aliens*—shows connecting religious writings to recent discoveries and questions. We bought books from Amazon, Barnes & Noble, and eBay. And Mat read each and every one and spearheaded the search.

Mat easily saw the connections in the resources that we might have otherwise overlooked, and he shared everything he found with us. It was reassuring and disconcerting at the same time. There was plenty of proof that Jake had experienced something related to what men had written about in the first and second centuries AD and much later, but that something—being in the kingdom of heaven and returning after speaking to God—was mind-blowing. It was absolutely paradigm-shifting.

It was wearing on Jake more and more. Being in the presence of God had been so intense, so amazing, so filling and powerful that being away from God was like being cast into hell. Jake craved God's presence the way an addict wants another hit, and between being separated from him and having so much unexplained stuff happening daily, it was soul-crushing.

Mat became so determined to help that he started reading superfast. He would hole up in his room and read for hours, absorbing information. He'd be up reading all night, obsessed with finding answers. Dante's *Inferno*, the *Book of Enoch*, the writings of Cephas, *The Key of Solomon the King*, and so many more related works began to fill our home. Mat's love of Roman history helped him splice historical moments and figures into what he was learning about the Bible. He believed firmly that every single word in his vast readings mattered.

Mat's fierce devotion to discovering the truth encouraged me early on to start reading the Bible too. In fact, we all started reading.

What we didn't immediately realize was that Mat was using his brilliant mind not only to try to understand what had happened to his brother but also to find and understand God. He was trying to prove the existence of God and discover God's origin and the origin of mankind's belief in God. My family had been placed on a path of discovery by a force far more powerful than we could comprehend. Unfortunately, that path was not an easy one to walk.

# Chapter 15

WHENEVER ONE OF us found something pertinent in one of the many books we were reading, we'd highlight it and share it with each other, discussing how one thing might relate to another. Finding things in ancient texts was the best! It was one thing for Jake to have experienced something like this, but then to know somewhere in the far past someone had written about it? It was like we'd been dropped into a totally different world. As much as we believed him, seeing that additional evidence was spectacular! Almost every night, we'd wind things down about an hour before bedtime by talking about what new information we'd learned.

As exciting as it was to find aspects of Jake's experience legitimized in ancient resources, it was also scary. If Jake's experience connected to something so ancient and powerful that long dead historians, philosophers, and men of religion had all written about it, maybe it was something even bigger, something not just connected to our family but to the entire world. Maybe it was important to all mankind. That was heavy.

Mat's fascination with learning and absorbing as much as he could got so bad I had to basically ground him. While some kids might be grounded because of their bad behavior and might lose the privilege to go do something fun, Mat's grounding was different. He was grounded because he was too deeply involved in research and, as a teen boy, he needed to live a little! As impressive as it was that he learned about the origins of the Catholic Church and the politics that led to the editing of the Bible and delved into writings regarding the Council of Nicaea and the ramifications of it, it wasn't healthy for him to disappear for hours upon hours reading everything he could. So as punishment, I forced him to play video games or watch mindless TV shows.

There was always something more to learn, more pieces of the puzzle to uncover and then put together. Without sports, and with his great sense of love and loyalty for his brother, Mat wasn't hanging out with his friends anymore; he was focused on Jake's and the family's needs.

We were learning so much and trying so hard! But I felt like I was losing my boys. Mat was forgetting to just *live* and enjoy, and Jake was struggling to just be here, a part of our world. We were in a desperate situation. I was certain I was watching my eldest boy become a recluse, while my baby boy died by degrees, wanting nothing but to be back in the presence of God. Not to say that he was suicidal—he wasn't—but he longed to be back with God so much that here, with us, he was gradually fading away.

Although my husband, Jay, was on the phone with our family as much as possible, his work schedule made it hard. He sneaked calls to me all the time. At work, he'd excuse himself to the bathroom and would call to check up on us. He knew we were struggling. I made that clear, but even working for his father, he had no leeway to come home and help, except on the weekends.

Family wasn't important the same way to Jay's dad as it was to Jay and to the rest of us.

The trouble was seeing firsthand what Jake was going through was completely different than hearing about it on the phone. Jay wasn't seeing what I was seeing, and I told him so.

To him, this was all coming out of left field. We'd nearly had it all. We'd been living the American dream, and then suddenly… boom! It was stolen from us. But for Jay, some of this was even harder to grasp because he was never around to witness it. He wasn't a big believer in anything religious—his dad had made it clear to him that anyone who believed in God or took part in religion was weak. He really had no background at all in anything connected to God.

While Jake struggled with having met God personally, Jay struggled with totally different parts of all this. He struggled with understanding what was happening. He struggled with not being home. Even being the breadwinner—providing our family's vital financial support—he couldn't be around to offer all the emotional support he desperately wanted to provide.

And it was the emotional support we all needed.

We argued. We fought. I needed more than he could provide. The kids needed more than he could give. He wanted to give more than work would allow.

When Jay and I couldn't see eye-to-eye or when work made him unavailable, Mat and I brainstormed. Mat picked up the slack, and we often talked about how to help Jake. Mat—so close to graduating high school and moving on—was mired in helping Jake. Mat sacrificed even more of what should have been the conclusion of a carefree childhood in order to help his family.

It was frustrating how much we had to change because of one chat with God. We had so many sleepless nights of being stalked and haunted by shadowy and demonic forces. We spent countless hours sitting in our home's stairwell praying and reading from the Bible in the loudest voice I could muster—all to drive away the darkness. How many hours, days, weeks, months of reading and research did we need to do before we could take control of our lives? How long could we withstand the many creepy moments of hearing our names called in our house by things that were both there and not there? How many more sleepless nights would I have of wondering when the next shoe would drop, wondering what else I could do, wondering what other ways I could keep my kids safe? It was all extremely exhausting.

Even with all the concerns I had about what my family was going through, the question I kept coming back to was, why us? We didn't ask for this. I had actively tried to avoid anything that might be even vaguely like this. It was all so strange and all too much. In the blink of an eye, we had gone from being a pretty typical all-American family, happy-go-lucky, socially active in our community and school, to seeking answers to much bigger questions and praying in self-defense.

Mat's remarkable devotion to his search for answers finally became overwhelming. I needed to keep my kids firmly attached to this world. I needed them in the here and now. I refused to have them stolen away by things existing in the afterlife, not without them having really lived their lives here first.

And I wasn't going to give up without a fight.

I needed Mat to back off a bit from his intense studying of religion and be a normal teenager since it was consuming his daily life. I forced him to come downstairs and relax. He had become so pale I made him go and lie out by the pool to catch some rays. I wanted him to have more family fun. More in this world, less obsessing over reading the next book. I realized our obsession for the truth was consuming us. I had to ground us in the physical world and distinguish the difference between living a regular life and a spiritual life. I tried my best to make everyone happy. Whenever I went grocery shopping, I stocked up on Jake's favorite foods to help give him something to look forward to. The amount of pepperoni pizza and wings we ate during that time? Wow. We had "family fun time" whenever Jay came home—weekends were for our whole family, for fun and adventure. The last thing I wanted to do was waste any of those precious moments.

But those little things mattered in big ways. I had grown up fighting for my own survival, figuring out what I needed to do to make it through each and every day. Looking back, I realize all that had helped prepare me for *this*. My childhood had been a tumultuous training ground for what was now clearly the main event. The fight of my life—and *for* my kids' lives.

The strange things we were experiencing in our own home never really completely stopped once they started but became consistent, even as we began to learn how to manage things better. From our reading and experience, we learned how to react when facing the worst of it: strange shadows and otherworldly voices became much more manageable. We began to sense when things were lurking in our house. We could feel when there was a dark presence or things were simply not right. The lesson God gave Jake on discerning between good and evil was tremendously useful. The feeling of your heart dropping into the pit of your stomach and the sense of dread never really went away; we just became more accustomed to what it meant. Try as we did, we hadn't managed to pray it away. So the kids and I gathered around our coffee table in the family room, knelt down, and held hands so nothing could break through while we prayed.

As I was asking the Lord to please watch over each child, protect our house, and give us guidance, I suddenly felt a sharp pain, like I had been stabbed in the back. An absolutely horrific sensation spread into my chest, surrounding my heart. It felt like invisible fingers wrapped around my heart and squeezed. I couldn't breathe. I wondered if this was what having a heart attack felt like. I struggled to get the words out and whispered to Mat, "Help me."

"Don't let it stop you," he urged. "Continue."

*Holy shit.* I could barely speak. I could barely get any air, so the rest of my prayer came out in a whisper. But it came out. And the pain slowly eased and evaporated.

I made an appointment with the cardiologist the next day. And a couple of days later, I went, got checked out, and discovered I had mitral valve prolapse. The doctor said my heart basically skips a beat about every eight beats. It was an arrhythmia and completely new to me. No one in my family had anything like it, and it was especially unnerving that it seemed to happen in the midst of our prayers, almost like something was trying to stop me from talking to God.

And if something was that determined—if something could do that to *me*—what could it do to my children?

I needed more support, more guidance in this battle we were waging. Even with everything I was doing, every stride forward I thought we were making, I was struggling. Bishop Jensen was still calling us from time to time to check in, still raising us up in prayer, still pushing for the kids to be baptized. "Baptism connects them to the Holy Spirit, Ali," he said. "And the Holy Spirit gives them a sort of spiritual armor that will help them deal with the things that keep coming their way."

I wanted my kids to have every weapon available to fight the things that kept wandering the halls and loitering in the rooms of our home. I wanted them to be protected. If it meant they had to be baptized, so be it. We'd get them baptized. I figured we had nothing to lose. Bishop had assured me that baptism was universal—it didn't force us to be tied to one particular church or any single narrow view of religion but would give us the protection of the Holy Spirit, and that protection would help the kids.

Jake always came to me first to tell me when something supernatural had happened, and one day, he took me aside and said he'd seen something odd in his sleep. "I was walking inside a building with concrete floors," he began. "There were other people with me. Five of us were walking forward in a formation, with two people on my right and two on my left. I was slightly ahead of them, leading our group, and I was wearing armor and holding a sword in my right hand. We were all wearing armor that looked similar, and I got the sense that it was to confuse the enemy—so the enemy didn't know which one I was. Ahead of us, built into the floor, was an empty cross-shaped baptismal font with stairs and silver railings leading down into it. We walked in silence, each of us knowing our roles and performing them with determination.

I had this intense and narrow focus, like I was hunting something. My eyes darted left and right, searching. We walked down the stairs into the empty baptismal font. When we reached its center, out of nowhere, a cold wind circled around me, and an icy wind fell upon us. It laughed and launched into the air, circling around to ambush us. The chilled wind pressed down on us with a brutal pressure, trying to bend us and force us down onto our knees. We all fought it, but one by one, my companions were forced to kneel, and their heads were forced to the ground. The pressure was intense, like a giant cold hand was shoving my head toward the floor. But I was determined. I was going to fight. And when I thought I might give in, I prayed. I asked God to give me strength, and suddenly, I was filled with it, and a light emanated from me. The wind and the creature accompanying it disappeared from the explosion of light bursting out of me, and my companions stood beside me again."

"What do you think it means?" I asked my son.

"I think it means I'm here for a reason. Like I have a job I have to do here, and I also have a job that could be part of what is happening now or at a different time. There's something big coming I have to deal with. Something I need to fight."

My heart pounded, both knowing and fearing that he was right.

"It's not going to be easy, Mom."

"No," I agreed.

"But that dream, that vision, it just reminds me that even though it's going to be hard, there will be good people with me. I'm not going to be fighting whatever this is alone."

I nodded. "No, Jake, you're absolutely right. You're not going to be alone in this. Not ever." I knew then that although Jake and I were both struggling with every dark and dangerous thing going on, we still had plenty of fight left in us.

We were fighters. We would battle on. Together.

# Chapter 16

THE BATTLE OUR family was fighting wouldn't be limited to one vision for Jake and not just to one visitation by something large and powerful. Much of what we were dealing with was both persistent and insidious. My frustration level seemed to constantly reach new peaks. As much as I had already achieved in my life—having come from nothing and fought for my very survival—as much as I was beginning to believe my violent and haunted childhood had, in ways, prepared me better than most to deal with dark and strange happenings, I still wasn't sure what else I could do to help my son win his particular war.

About seven months after Jake's first vision, he had an even more disturbing vision. He explained to me that it was as if he was on a train, riding through a park. The train—which was, in some ways, more like a roller coaster on a track—entered a building where the doors popped open to reveal images that seemed to be straight out of fairy tales. It then carried Jake forward and into another building. The train stopped, and Jake stepped out. The structure he stepped into had pillars, a podium, and rows of chairs. It looked like an old church.

As Jake walked to the podium, he noticed a book. It was made of flesh and laid open. There was at first a familiarity to it. It was almost like reading a Bible, but the words twisted into things he knew in his heart were lies—lies so wrong and bad that his stomach soured inside of him. Upon recognizing this, Jake saw through the illusion of the church. The light through the windows turned red and gave everything an eerie crimson glow. The chairs were made of flayed and contorted but living flesh. The walls, which should have been constructed of large stone blocks, were instead made of living human flesh, and blood created a grim and gory coating for the floor, crafting a grotesque parody of a religious setting.

Before him, a black mist began to form, rising and solidifying, shaping itself into hands.

Jake cried out, "Oh my god!"

Laughing, the shadowy figure said, "Thou shalt not take my father's name in vain" and sprang toward him. Jake managed to raise one fist to fight before he suddenly woke up, back in his bed but badly shaken.

Each time a dark vision came to Jake, it lingered like a pit in his gut that made him feel sick and sorrowful for a few days afterward. It would cloud his mind, making him feel slow and heavy. He'd struggle to function normally as his mind just kept rolling through the images he'd seen, not wanting to relive his time in that strange and unsettling place but unable to pull completely free as he tried to parse some meaning. Sometimes it took Jake a week to mentally clear out what he'd seen and felt, and I watched it continue to wear him down.

I took him to have physicals done, and nothing seemed out of the ordinary—except for the way he'd come home from an average school day completely depleted and collapse onto his bed to nap. There were days, between visions, when I'd pick him up from school for lunch and he'd sit in the car with me and pour his heart out, in tears, and other days he just sat silently and ate his lunch. It was in those moments that it was hardest to be his mom. I didn't know what else to do. Whatever was going on was absolutely engulfing him, and I seemed helpless to do anything but watch it slowly destroy my boy. I needed to stop it.

I did what I could. I kept things light at home and tried to bring fun into everything we did. Not only were Jake's visions taking a toll on him, they were still wearing away at our entire family. Mat and I talked a lot about how best to keep Jake in the here and now, functioning in *this* world and not being pulled away by the visions he was seeing. We knew we had to keep him living *here*, regardless of what was happening on the other side in the world to come. No matter what we did, though, whatever we had to offer him here on the physical plane, nothing could compare with his time walking with God. He missed him so much it was like a wound that never healed.

I learned to fight even better by using Scripture. I—the girl who hated religion—prayed nearly nonstop now. I wasn't part of any strictly organized religion—we weren't attending any church—but I was growing closer to God, whether I wanted to or not. I laid my hands on Jake's head and prayed for God to bless and protect him. I prayed in the hallway outside his door whenever he was inside his bedroom. I read Scripture out loud, seated on the stairs at all hours of the night, willing my voice to act as a shield for my family. And I was terrified almost the entire time I did any and all of it.

But together, through trial, error, a lot of reading and pure faith, our family was able to find some semblance of peace, and we began to take more control of our lives.

Shortly after his second vision, during that period in which evil and darkness gathered, Jake had started drifting off to sleep when something formed up in his vision in the same way the wildly popular 3D posters of the nineties created an image when your eyes finally relaxed. A creature came into view. It had a powerful man's body and a distinct and highly decorative sort of armor plating that gave the impression it was worn by royalty. Jake's eyes drifted up, noticing that above the human skin of the man's chest, the flesh grew a sickeningly pale color, and the beast's anatomy changed. As Jake's gaze continued to rise, the neck that should have logically been human became bovine, and he met the eyes of what he recognized from mythology to be something like a minotaur. It was hairless, though, only covered in sickly white skin, with big black soulless eyes rimmed in a pale red. Its snout dripped snot, and on either side of its head grew two wicked-looking horns, one broken. Between them was a floating busted golden crown.

Original painting by Cydney in collaboration with Jake of Moloch

Jake recognized it immediately as not simply from the mytho-logical Greek labyrinth but something much more grim. A name he had never read or heard before invaded his mind: Moloch.

Even more frightening, although it distinctly seemed closer to humans than the beast standing before Jake, was the person—the man—who stood behind and to the left of the monster, wearing a hooded robe. Jake knew immediately that the one who looked most human was actually the most monstrous. The man's shoulders rolled forward a bit, providing him with a slightly hunched appear-ance, and Jake got the impression he was somehow both angelic and broken. His robe was open at the chest, and a slash of bright white marked him with a savage scar. Even though the upper part of his face was hidden in the hood's shadows, there was something darkly angelic about him and the perfect smirk twisting his mouth.

The chill that raced through Jake told him that he wasn't only in the presence of Moloch but standing far too close for comfort to Satan himself.

Jake jolted awake and raced to my room to tell me everything.

The next day, we again dug into research, and Mat found Moloch, looking just as Jake had described as Jake had known his name instinctively. Moloch was not just any minotaur or bull. Instead, he was a Canaanite god connected to child sacrifice by fire and, in ancient times, had a significant cult following in the ancient Middle East.

Not only had Jake walked with God and visited his throne room. Now it seemed that the devil had demanded an introduction too.

It was all a lot to carry. It was hard enough managing three kids—as good as they were—and running a household with a husband who was working so hard he was only home on weekends. To add everything else on top of it, regardless of what Bishop said about telling no one, I needed to talk to someone for the sake of my own mental health. I knew that if I wasn't in a good headspace, I couldn't possibly be the mother and wife—the vital support system—that my family needed.

I confided in a couple we'd met: Stan and his wife, Maggie. Stan was an attorney who very much wanted to believe in a god but needed proof, and Maggie was a Mormon with another nearby ward. Our daughters had become friends, and we invited their entire family over for dinner one day. I didn't intend to tell them about Jake and his visions. I didn't intend to share anything weird. We were just going to eat some good food, chat, and let the kids run around a bit wild.

It was going to be a barbecue like any other normal family had. Or so I thought.

As Maggie and I were standing outside on the patio watching the kids playing on the trampoline and having a great time, I noticed Maggie was looking all around the yard as if she'd spotted something strange. She suddenly asked me, "Ali, can we go inside?"

I knew from her tone she didn't mean just the two of us.

"Sure," I said. I grabbed Cydney and hustled everyone back inside, curious as to what Maggie's reasoning was. "Everything okay?"

Maggie looked at me, and I realized she was pale. "You have spirits walking around your yard." She said it with a straight face and such certainty and conviction it was plain she just expected me to believe her.

"What?"

"Out there," she said, "I saw dark spirits moving around your backyard."

"Huh," I said. "Wanna help set the table?" I wanted to spill my guts, but as much as I wanted to, I needed to know the person I was talking to was ready to really hear what I had to say. And that they wouldn't think I—or my family—was crazy.

We ate dinner, successfully avoiding any discussion about the supernatural during mealtime.

But after dinner, the weirdness ramped back up when Maggie asked, "Why are your kids so perfect?"

I looked at them. "I don't know," I said. To me, they just naturally behaved that way.

"They're so kind," she said, "so polite."

I shrugged. They were good kids.

"Is there something going on with your family? There's just—" She paused. "There's something strange about your boys."

She waited for me to respond, but I stayed quiet. What could I say? Yeah, the one saw God, and the other read the entire Bible in, like, two weeks, and they fought invisible shadow monsters. But it's not like I could tell them that, right? There's just something different about them, isn't there?"

*Ugh.* Was she normal? I really looked at her. Could she be trusted? Maybe she was crazy enough to believe in me. I decided to take a chance. She seemed up to believing in the supernatural. "Well," I said, "the kids have been trying to find God. And we've been reading and studying religious books to find him," I admitted.

Overhearing us, Stan perked right up. "I want to know about God," he said. "Tell me what you've learned." His excitement was contagious, but Jake hesitated, caught like a deer in headlights.

Since Jake wasn't ready to talk much about what he was discovering, Mat, our resident scholar, immediately dove into research mode. He explained some of the history and discussed the books we were reading, what we'd been discovering, and what we thought it all might mean. Throughout it all, we managed to remain cautious—not saying too much—but it felt great to share! Stan, having been an atheist, was particularly interested in the things we had to say and asked a lot of questions. He wanted to know if God existed.

"Since you've learned so much and believe," Stan said, "would you give me a prayer? Maybe this will help me come to know if there really is some god after all. I sure haven't been able to find God by myself."

The youngest of their kids had been racing around, screaming and playing, but it seemed they were briefly muted at that moment. I looked at both the boys and at Jay.

Everyone seemed okay with it. "We've never done that before," I pointed out. "But why not? We'll get Jake to do it."

Jake said, "Sure."

"Great!" Stan said.

All of us but Maggie and the younger kids went upstairs. We pulled out a chair for Stan. Jake gently laid his hands on Stan's head, like he'd seen Bishop Jensen do in the past, and the rest of us placed ours on top of his head as we'd seen done when Bishop Jensen gave a prayer. At only fourteen, Jake began his first prayer. It was quiet and peaceful at first, just a boy's blessing weaving its way through the air, asking politely for God's attention. The room became warm, and then really warm, and Jake's childish self suddenly disappeared as if he had become a much more mature and sophisticated person—someone wise beyond his years.

The atmosphere changed, thickening, and Jake said, "Oh, hi, God."

There was a sweetness in the room, a gentle, loving presence filling the space, and I started to cry—it was like nothing I had ever felt, except once before. Jay was visibly shaken, and Stan fell to the floor and began to sob. We lingered in that silent space for a moment, and then the vital power that had filled the room was whisked away, and we reached down to help Stan up.

Even with all of us helping, it was a struggle to lift Stan back to his feet. He'd become dead weight and was crying so loudly that Maggie rushed up the stairs and burst into the room. Stunned, she got the kids together and piled the family into the car. It was a strange goodbye, certainly not the way any of us had expected a barbecue with friends to end!

A week later, Maggie called and asked, "So what really happened up there?" She was completely out of sorts and needed answers. Since his blessing by Jake, Stan had grown so despondent that he couldn't bring himself to go into work for an entire week. Though the body-wracking sobs had ended, he still couldn't stop crying and hadn't left his bed in a week.

I didn't know what to do or what to say. I had only wanted to open up a little bit to people we thought we could trust, but some divine intervention swept Stan away. I decided that for Stan's, Maggie's, and their children's safety, I would push them away, regardless of how much we could have used some good, solid friends. It was clear Stan couldn't handle what happened in Jake's prayer and, for the sake of his job and his family, it was the best for him.

Protecting Jake was also on my mind as it was always.

From that point on, I realized that I had to be much more cautious as to whom we spoke to and with whom we could share the things that we learned. The supernatural happenings in the house continued. The voices calling our names, the lingering and shifting shadows…dark figures would suddenly gather and speed across our field of vision…giant figures would be spotted standing in our stairways, watching us.

Such things became routine, standard moments making up "just another day" in the Crawford household. Creepy as it was, some of it we could simply dismiss as being part of our dreadful "new normal."

Having fought these unexplained happenings without the help of another adult, the only consistent outside support I got was from Jay. Jay called all the time—any chance he got. It would've been bothersome the way he was always checking up on us, if it hadn't been so appreciated. If not for his calls, there would have been no one else I could talk to about what was happening in the house.

Bishop Jensen received a new position in the church, requiring much more of his time. He could not help us as much as he once did. Although he believed in Jake's vision and still insisted that Jake would see more from God, he said if anything else happened, we should call him right away, and he would make time for us.

Personally, I became more convinced that my crappy childhood had given me a head start on what was happening now. I was convinced that this was some horrible test we had to pass. Why my family was chosen to participate in this spiritual SAT, I had no idea. I just knew that together as a family, we were kicking ass. If only the poltergeist pop quizzes would give us a break! But all the research we were doing on God and religion was starting to raise new questions for us.

# Chapter 17

WHEN WE DUG into the Apocryphal books—which the Mormons were staunchly against reading, but Bishop Jensen was okay with us exploring—the question that most often came to mind was why had these books been trimmed from the Bible or never initially inserted into it? This question caused Mat to do more than just read more broadly but go extensively into the history of the books and time periods in which they were written. Mat needed more than faith that the books were real; he needed evidence. Why was it written? Who wrote it? When was it written? Who talked about it? Where was it written? How many times was it written or rewritten? What was the earliest record in which the book had been mentioned?

Mat dove into every book with a healthy degree of skepticism that made him examine them critically. The expanded literature told similar stories and in similar tones to the early biblical writings, and some seemed really pertinent to what we were struggling with. At the time of their writing, and in certain cases, when Jesus walked the earth and even later, the books were considered important to having an understanding of God and to the emergence of religious thought and organized religion's structure. If those books were important for Jesus's reading and education, why exclude them now? If Jesus made a reference from a book outside of the Bible, why not study the book Jesus made reference to? As Mat discovered through hours, days, weeks, and months (and at this point, it's been years) of research, far too often, the reason was politics.

Organized religion was often political—emperors and kings used riches and war much the same way religious leaders pressured emperors and kings with the promise of heaven, and the threat of hell pressured religious leaders. Over time, the content of the Bible began to change. Mat noticed that the King James version of the Bible had less books in it than the Catholic version, and the Catholic version had fewer books in it than the Septuagint or Greek version of the Bible, Greek Orthodoxy being from the same religious origin as Roman Emperor Constantine, who ordered the Bible be compiled at the Council of Nicaea. Politics most often served a particular and well-established hierarchy much more than it served the will of God. It felt like we were potentially at a crossroads: we wanted the support of organized religion but a broader view of writings and research than most organized religions happily provided. Most of all, we wanted answers to how to protect our family from the strange happenings that seemed nearly ever-present.

One day, as Jake was playing video games in Cydney's room, he saw a little girl walk into his peripheral vision. She was about eight years old and had a sweet look about her. She wore a pretty white dress, and when he turned his head to look at her more directly, she started bouncing a ball. Jake thought, *Huh*, and paused for a moment while he processed the situation. Then he said firmly, "If you are good, you can stay, but if you're bad, you have to leave."

With that, she disappeared, and he never saw her again. He returned to playing his game. Such brief visitations had become almost routine—Jake was always catching glimpses of things and was no longer as easily shaken. He'd learned to not acknowledge anything too directly because that seemed to feed it, giving it power. So if any of us was concerned about something that showed up, we'd cast it out immediately. And if things became too bothersome for Jake, he'd come to me and I'd walk through each room in our family's home, saying prayers and cleaning things out that way. Keeping our place clean required a much different set of tools than a broom, mop, and bucket.

As much good as those sorts of efforts did, the thing we still lacked was the power of the Holy Spirit, which Bishop Jensen felt

127

would give our family an additional ability to deal with demons and related entities. But acquiring such a powerful gift from God required the kids to get baptized, and in order to be baptized, the kids had to be educated by whichever church they would be baptized in. Although Jensen had made it clear earlier that baptism didn't strictly tie you to any particular church because we wanted him to perform the baptism, and he wanted to do it, the kids needed to learn the Mormon requirements.

I finally decided to bite the bullet and call Bishop Jensen, saying we were ready to begin the process so he could baptize us, and I made it clear that he was the only one we trusted to do it. He already knew that when everything was said and done, what we wanted for our family was not the Mormon church, but the protection he assured us we would get with baptism—and particularly for Jake—was the highest level of spiritual protection and the best possible guidance for him. He was also very aware that to be baptized, the kids needed to attend church services and be visited and instructed by missionaries in certain religious teachings. We did not want to go to the Mormon church. Bishop Jensen understood why we would not want to go to the old ward or the Mormon church. He even said the old ward was sick with too much money and drama and was not a good example of what the Mormon church was. He pleaded with us to go to a different ward so we could see what he saw in the Mormon church and to give it an honest go. He said a new ward would give us a fresh start and hopefully prove to us one way or another if the Mormon church was true.

"Take it easy in the new ward. Relax, go in with an open heart—each ward is different in almost the same way each Christian church is different. They all have their own personalities in a way. Go to sacrament incognito, as it were, keep your heads down, and ease into things at the new ward. I really want this to work out for you."

"Okay," I said, "we can do that."

As awful as the Mormon church had been to us, I trusted and respected Bishop Jensen. He helped us with the passing of my father; he warned us that something bad was going to happen with the church; he even said that something special was going to happen to our family, and it did. I decided to place my trust in him once more and go give another Mormon ward a try. If so many churches were Mormon, then I thought maybe there was something I could learn from it.

Boy, was I wrong.

About a month later, I decided I'd put things off long enough. It was time to attend sacrament with the new ward and see if Bishop was right. Jay wouldn't go with us; he hated the idea of going to a religious service we didn't even believe in. The church certainly wasn't winning him over. He also saw what the stress of all this was doing to us. Although the new ward was a distinct entity from our previous ward, it met in the same building—just at a different time. We had to go in between ward services because, otherwise, the old ward's members—people we wanted no contact with—might be walking the halls. The odds of bumping into members of our old ward were high in that building or going to or from it, and I didn't want to deal with any of their drama. Talk about stress! I hoped those horrible people had either moved on or that they'd grown up and become better people during our absence, but I had my doubts.

Standing just outside, I eyed the place, my heart full of misgivings. Mat took my hand in his and led our family inside to an empty spot on a pew near the back, characteristically late.

It was a typical sacrament service in most ways. There was prayer, singing, reflection, and witnessing. But when one man stood up to witness, I noticed a distinct difference between this ward and our old one. He talked about how lucky he was. He mentioned he'd recently been in a serious car accident and broken his hip, and now he was absolutely penniless. But he was still grateful because he was still here—still alive and still *here*—sharing in Christian fellowship with good people. That's when it really hit me. How very different this ward was from the previous one. This new ward was humble.

These weren't Mormons who owned law firms and lived in mega mansions, but Mormons who lived in condos and modest homes and appeared to behave more like normal people. It was cool and humbling to be there; although our family weren't the wealthiest in our community, we were still most often running with the high society crowd, and there were different expectations, expectations that we would want more and strive hard to get more. We'd seen some people attempt to build their wealth and power through questionable means, like the Allure Foundation and its shady dealings. There'd even been a time a wealthy church member had visited our home and asked me why I stayed with Jay when she could introduce me to wealthier men, and I could have an even bigger house and even fancier cars…if I just abandoned Jay.

Needless to say, she was not invited back to our home. But in this ward, things felt much different. I watched how members of the congregation treated each other, looking for the little things that spoke volumes about a place and its people. I watched for the way people smiled or didn't, the way they shared hymnals, the way they guided their kids during the service. These people didn't seem to be competing or striving to gain some special status or recognition but were earnestly interested in each other and in being good people. These were everyday folks trying to get a little closer to God.

Still, "fool me once, shame on you, fool me twice…" I wasn't ready to commit just yet.

As the last prayer of sacrament closed, I whispered to the kids, "Now go!" And together we bolted out the door and headed for the car. Suddenly we heard the new bishop shout for us, saying, "Hey, guys, hey!" We stopped, and hesitantly, I turned around to face him. He was a dozen feet or more away from us and said, "Please. Don't be afraid."

I wasn't sure how to respond or if any response was necessary.

"You're welcome here anytime."

I nodded slowly, knowing the kids were watching. But I wouldn't make any promises for us—I didn't guarantee we'd be back, not next week or any other.

He seemed to understand. "I'll welcome you back next week," he assured me, adding, "It was so nice to have you here." He offered us a kind smile, said, "Goodbye," and returned to the congregation.

That next week, we got a call from Bishop Jensen, asking how our first experience at the new ward was. I thought it was a little weird that he knew we'd gone, but I paid it no mind. I said that the ward seemed nice, and we briefly talked to its bishop and he seemed nice. Bishop Jensen was glad that we'd taken the first steps on the path toward baptism.

He said that after our last conversation, he had called the bishop of the new ward we were attending. This was news to me; I'd had no idea. He said, "I told him a little about you and your family, and I told him about Jake's vision and the trouble we had gone through with the prior ward." This pissed me off a bit because he had told me not to tell anyone, yet he was telling people without me knowing!

Now I knew why the bishop of the new ward tracked us down and told us not to be afraid. I felt a bit like a freak. Bishop Jensen explained that he wanted to ease our transition into the new ward and knew this bishop, and he was a good person. I understood what Bishop Jensen was doing, but it put me in an awkward position.

Amid the ongoing strange happenings at our house that week, I mulled over our return to that ward, and encouraged by the new bishop's words, we attended sacrament the next Sunday too. After sacrament, I met with the new ward bishop in his office, and he confirmed that he talked with Bishop Jensen and wanted to protect Jake. He reassured me that he believed Jake and was willing to do anything in his capacity to help. We felt genuinely welcomed and started to like the place and its people. The kids were nicer there too. We all got along well.

In time, we made friends and started slowly opening up to people, but, honestly, if it hadn't been for the promise of the power of the Holy Spirit, we wouldn't have wasted our time on any ward. Yes, the people at the new ward were great. But we were only there to get help. Bishop Jensen had assured us the Holy Spirit was vital to dealing with demonic forces, and we hoped what we were doing to earn it was worth it. Like any mother, I wanted my kids as safe and as well protected as possible. If that meant getting the Holy Spirit, so be it. If getting the Holy Spirit required baptism (which Bishop assured us it did), we'd get the kids baptized. If it required Bishop Jensen to have permission from the church to baptize the kids, which in turn meant attending church services and having missionaries come and instruct the kids, we'd make that happen too.

We had a goal almost all parents share: to protect our kids. Our kids, though, required an extra level of spiritual protection that, thankfully, few ever do. So although I carefully timed things so we entered sacrament late and left early, we were doing everything that was technically required of us. Ultimately, I wanted my kids baptized, and then we could get the heck out of that church. Although we reluctantly became more active in the church, I hoped people in the church could somehow help Jake. After all, Bishop Jensen knew things we didn't, and what he'd predicted had come true.

Surely, not all wards could be as bad as the old one, right?

I let Bishop, know what we were doing. We gave the church a go, giving it a few months to get the ball rolling in the new ward with the goal of baptism. I reported that the kids felt safe, and I was mostly managing to avoid the monstrous men and women from our previous ward who sometimes strutted the building's halls between services and classes.

We became regular attendees, attending sacrament regularly, as we had agreed with Bishop Jensen. Feeling comfortable with the polite curiosity and honest warmth shown to our family, we gradually attended a few Sunday school sessions. Even on the days we'd stay for Sunday school, we never fully committed for the whole three hours. God or no God, that felt like it was asking way too much! Besides, Jay was only home on weekends, and we wanted as much time with him as possible. After all, wasn't family number one? Didn't everyone say how important the family was? We were well on our way to doing what was required to get the kids baptized and having them better protected.

For a while, things continued going really well until, suddenly, they weren't.

Three weeks into becoming comfortable at our new ward, our new bishop asked me to meet him at his office because there were some things we needed to talk about. I went there with my heart in my throat. Sitting down across from him in his office, I could see he was visibly upset. After a little small talk, he began, "I'm so sorry. The stake president has said that your children are never to say a prayer, never to speak up, not to answer any questions or ask any questions.

They are never to give their testimony. They are never to read aloud in classes or to participate in any way." His voice was cracking.

Anger boiled up inside of me. Our old ward had viciously attacked our friends and forced them out, and now they were... what? Punishing children for doing what? What had my children done to be ostracized? They weren't even members of the church. They were still "investigators." Weren't investigators allowed to ask questions and to try and understand what they were teaching? Or did they just want us to follow blindly and never ask a single question? It all made me feel sick.

"This is...upsetting," he admitted. "Your family is not to have any callings or to help people in any way." He was absolutely distraught. "I've met your children. They're good kids. Kind, polite, solid. They are only children." He paused to catch his breath. "I didn't see anything wrong or evil in your children. They were knowledgeable and always enhanced deeper discussion that got the whole class excited and involved." His voice grew grave when he said, "I talked with Bishop Jensen. He is a wise man and a good man. Ali"—he paused again, letting his words gather weight—"I believe Jake, and I believe your kids are good. They do not deserve what is being done to them."

"All I know is that my kids have seen some strange shit. Jake has been through a lot, and my kids haven't done anything to the Mormon church to be treated this way. All I want is for my kids to get some help. I'm not asking for a lot. I'm just asking for help. I need them to be safe. Baptism is supposed to offer him protection."

"And that's what we're going to do—keep him as safe as possible. So I'm going to make an exception for Jake: rather than divide the kids up for their classes here because of their ages, I want Mat to stick to Jake like glue. He'll be with him the whole time. Jake will never be left alone."

"Really?" Even after all the bad news, all the constraints, this was something. "Thank you."

"Ali," he said, "we value your family and can see there's something special about those kids of yours. I know this all is frustrating—I've never faced a situation like this before, but please let us help you help them."

I nodded. Even if the stake president was trying to control us, at least we were with people who earnestly cared for us, and we were still on the path to baptism and additional security. In that, at least, I had reasons to hope.

# Chapter 18

THE WEIRD OCCURRENCES haunting us at home started following Jake to school. One day, a classmate did something really bizarre. Jake's class had a substitute teacher that day, and there was a stretch of personal reading time, during which all of the kids were supposed to take out a book. The substitute was pretty hands-off, creating a relaxed atmosphere, and although Jake had taken out something of his own, this boy who sat near Jake turned around and handed him an open book, pointing to a particular section and telling Jake to read it.

While the kids scattered throughout the classroom studied, read, and chatted with each other like on any other day with an unconcerned sub, Jake moved the book so it was easily in view. He had no reason to suspect anything weird was going on; maybe this kid had found a particularly interesting, funny, or shocking excerpt to share. So Jake started reading. He zipped through the passage pretty quickly but was stunned to discover he'd read a paragraph that essentially said that by reading it, the reader had become the possession of Satan. Yes. The book claimed that by reading that portion, you had entered into a contract with the devil, and now your soul belonged to him. Jake, like many kids his age, had read it before he'd totally understood what it was he was reading. He was shocked. This random classmate of his started jumping up and down with glee, and with thunderous laughter, he started saying, "*We* got you, *we* got you!" His howling laughter filled the classroom.

And *that* was when the really odd part happened. Not far away, in the same classroom, a girl stood up and walked straight over to stand by Jake's side. This girl wasn't a friend of Jake's; she'd never expressed any interest in him. She wasn't even a girl Jake really knew—Jake paid her so little attention that he barely recognized her as being a classmate at all. This girl strode over, looked at the book, and then at the boy who'd passed it to Jake. "Leave Jake alone."

The boy stopped laughing, took back his book, and sat quietly at his desk as if nothing had ever happened. The girl returned to her desk as quickly as she had walked over. The whole experience raced through Jake's mind—he had no idea what to make of it.

When Jake told me about everything that had transpired, I chalked it up as another unexplained event. But unlike dozens of other strange things he'd managed to shake off, this clearly bothered Jake. This bizarre experience with a random stranger, who knew nothing about what Jake had otherwise experienced and had handed Jake a book that would give his soul to Satan, was way out there. This hadn't happened at home nor had it happened at church. In fact, it was divorced from anything to do with religion. It had happened in Jake's classroom, where a random stranger had brought the supernatural to Jake in a bizarre and terrifying manner.

Jake had his third vision when he was fourteen and a freshman in high school. It followed the destruction he'd seen begin in his first vision, when the earth was set ablaze by fire, falling from the sky. Standing there in the vision, on an earth that had been all but destroyed by fire and facing the ruins of our family home, Jake got the distinct impression that he and Mat were already dead. Above him, the sky was bloodred and ominous. Jake watched from a distance as, not far outside the rubble of our house, his father found Mat's and Jake's bodies. Jay lovingly buried them side by side, marking the two graves with wooden crosses, each cross bearing one of the boys' names.

Original painting by Cydney in collaboration
with Jake of his vision of the graves

As Jay knelt, crying, between the graves of our sons, a huge figure in a black, hooded robe that was as dark as a starless sky, appeared before Jay and reached out a bony hand toward the crosses. Fire leaked from the specter's fingertips as it slowly scorched the names off of both crosses, determined to frighten Jay and convince him that there was no hope. Soulless as it was, it was hungry to show him that both his children and their efforts would be forgotten nearly as soon as they were dead. It was yet another vision that shook Jake and caused him to be out of sorts for the next few days. But as frightening as it was, Jake also knew it was false and not sent by God but something much darker and more dangerous.

At church, my children's imposed silence began. All around us, ward members volunteered to share a prayer or give testimony about their belief in either God, Jesus, or the teachings of Joseph Smith—or all three. When we'd pile back into the car to return home, occasionally, one of my kids would mention someone doing something in Sunday school or someone asking a question. But had my children been allowed to do anything of the sort? No. If they had questions, could they ask them in the church? No. It was absolutely unfair.

And yet without a church official answering them, they had to consider their questions more carefully, and we would sometimes discuss things as a family.

They took that uncomfortable situation, combined it with their keen research skills, and continued to develop as deep and spiritual thinkers.

We weren't the only ones in the ward who were discouraged by the situation. The friends we'd recently made at the new ward started asking questions when they realized something was happening, too, and to them, it also seemed like we were being unjustly targeted by the Mormon church. They had also never seen anything quite like it, and it made them nervous. Why would a church that claimed to be a true church of God—their church—be so determined to maneuver and bully a family? Why would a few of the stake's leading men be so intent on such a thing? Unfortunately, I had no good nor easy answer to give our friends.

In an attempt to understand the choice our old ward had made, a choice that was clearly unlike any the church was known to have previously made, our new ward's bishop stopped by the house to visit a few times. He wanted to see the kids just being kids, wanted to know if there was something he'd somehow missed when assessing our family—something dark the stake president had glimpsed and felt only he could control. But each visit at our home concluded with him thanking me for my hospitality and giving me a perplexed and sad shake of his head. "I just don't get it," he admitted. "They're just kids. Your kids are being targeted. It makes me question so much."

I couldn't help but agree and on all three of his points.

"I'd take this straight to the Salt Lake authorities—nothing about this feels right or good," he admitted. "Who attacks children like this? Because that's what this is—an attack on children by denying them church services. Yes, I'd take this to Salt Lake if I was you. You need to keep fighting."

I nodded. But I didn't want to keep fighting. I was already fighting every day against things that were paranormal—why did I need to fight against people in the church that I'd gone to for help? I didn't want to take the fight to Salt Lake City, but it was a good idea.

Bishop Jensen and Jay coauthored a letter to Salt Lake. I just wanted the kids baptized. How hard was that supposed to be?

We attended for nearly three months, and although I'm not sure what, if anything, the new bishop had said to anyone after our talks about the restrictions my children were under, several older men came up to me at different points and urged me not to stop fighting on behalf of my children. They were determined that I should make sure my children received the services the church should provide them. I took each suggestion graciously and humbly. So it wasn't startling when one day, another older man grabbed me by the arm as we were leaving the church and demanded, "Don't you stop fighting. Fight for your children." Like every other time, I nodded, muttered some words of thanks, and thought very little of it afterward.

That is, until I realized a couple days later that the man who had grabbed my arm and had spoken directly to me had died the week before in a bicycle crash. Then I gave things a little more thought. In both this world and the next, people—or spirits that looked and felt like people—wanted me to get the kids baptized. There had to be something to it.

Then, almost exactly three months into our time with the new ward, our new bishop stopped us from entering the church one Sunday. He explained, "I have been ordered to deny you at the door. You are not allowed to come back to church unless you attend your original ward." Pulling me aside, he added, "I believe Jake is talking to God and I'm doing everything possible to help. Please believe me. But you can't stay, Ali. I'm so sorry. I can't let you or the kids in. I was told that I could not approve of your children being baptized," he continued. "They told me that so long as you went to this ward, I could not send missionaries to your house nor could I conduct the interviews for the kids to get baptized. I'm sorry, but I've been told to deny any baptism request. I'm sorry, there's nothing I can do." He concluded with, "This has never happened before. I've never heard of anything like this. I've never seen this before."

The bishop was clearly upset, knowing what he was doing was wrong, but he followed the orders he was given. He would follow his leaders even though he knew it was wrong. I had been given an ultimatum: to receive baptism, my children, who were investigating the church, must go to the place the church leaders told us to go, go at the times they told us to, and follow every word coming from their mouths blindly. There would be no questions asked.

It was absolute bullshit. This was not for me—if it had been, I would have just stayed with my mother.

Regardless of what Bishop told us, was it worth this much hard work to get baptized in a church that seemingly wanted to dictate every action in our lives? Didn't Mormons baptize everyone, including dead people? Why would I need to go back to the old ward when things were going so well in this one? Did we really need to jump through even more hoops to get baptized? We would be giving up our freedom, our free will. I needed to be away from that church, regain control of our own lives, and reassess what baptism really meant. Perhaps the price for protection was just too great.

One day, Jake said a prayer while seated at his desk in school. He asked God to let him know who his enemies were so he could avoid them. It seemed like an easy enough thing to ask God for, but Jake had no idea how God would show him the truth of people. In the hallway, Jake watched the way some people's faces morphed, slipping out of their normal, human appearance, and into something twisted and wrong. He started to notice that people who weren't close to God had demons walking beside them and whispering to them—influencing their choices and slipping into their skins to possess them. And most horrific of all, the people they were possessing had no idea what was going on.

Jake knew, though, and it chilled him to realize how blind other people could be to what was influencing their behavior and making their choices for them. There had to be a way to make things better—for everyone.

School became increasingly rough on Jake, and his Spanish teacher realized something big was troubling him. The man took him aside one day as he was getting ready to leave the classroom and said, "Hey, I've noticed you've gotten a lot quieter in class recently."

Jake just looked at him and didn't say a word—basically proving his teacher's point.

"Anyhow," the man continued, "if anything's going on in your life, and you need a place to go to get away from it, you can come and sit in here during lunch."

"Thanks," Jake said. "I will."

And Jake did, but even before he took him up on that kind offer, his teacher reached out to me and let me know what he was seeing in Jake's behavior. And after he mentioned Jake being quiet and not quite like himself and that he'd offered him a safe place to come to, he got a little quiet and added, "Mrs. Crawford—"

"Yes?"

"I'm a pretty religious guy."

"Okay."

"And I wanted to let you know that there's definitely something going on with your boy." He gave a big sigh and then continued. "Whenever I look at him, I see this really bright light. It's all around him. Like an aura. Or a halo."

"Umm…okay," I said.

"I just wanted you to know. He's a good kid, but there's definitely something going on with him."

"Thank you for calling and letting me know," I said. What else could I say? I didn't want another situation like Stan's, and I wasn't interested in confiding in someone new about Jake's visions.

The supernatural hardship was not limited to just the boys; Cydney had her fair share of trouble as well. A worrisome situation happened to her at school one day. As much as I hated the problems we experienced at home, in some ways, I was even angrier about the ones that occurred at school. One day, in the school's large library, Cydney and my best friend's daughter Rachel were sitting down together, reading and laughing like young girls do, when something screamed "Cydney!" in a deep and demonic voice that stopped both of the young girls' laughter dead. They looked at each other, wide-eyed, and Cydney glanced around the immediate area and quickly dismissed the voice as strange but nothing dangerous enough to worry about.

She said, "Well, that's not normal," and then went back to reading and chatting.

Her friend, however, began to cry uncontrollably. She had never dealt with these sorts of things. Cydney had grown up being haunted. Cydney told me all about it, and that night, as she lay in bed, I laid my hands on her head and prayed that God would watch over her. At peace, knowing that I'd asked for God's protection on her behalf, Cydney slept well.

However, a couple days later, my best friend, Rachel's mom, called. Since meeting her in our first ward when our girls became friends, I'd talked to her pretty often and pretty honestly. She knew about Jake's visions and a ton of the weird happenings that had become our norm. Looking back, she was the best sort of friend anyone dealing with stuff like this could have—one who understood and believed without needing to see any of the frightening stuff up close and personal. And someone who laughed her way through it.

"Rachel's sleeping in our bed. What the heck happened to our girls?" she asked with a laugh. She was always so upbeat—fun and funny—if only more people were like her!

"I don't know," I told her. "They heard some sort of deep voice." We started laughing about it. It was all so bizarre!

"Was your kid freaked out by it?"

"Nope."

"So what do we do?" she asked. "I love her, but she can't keep sleeping in our bed. She's too old for that."

All I knew was that between nearly every breath I took—whether I was cooking, cleaning, reading, picking up or dropping off the kids—I tried to keep God in my heart. Like Jake and Mat made so plain through their actions, I also believed God would not abandon us, especially not after speaking to Jake. God didn't need me to wait until I was in church or with a bishop to talk to him. He was always ready and able to hear me out. And by reaching out to God, I knew I was doing *something*. Maybe other people needed to understand that too. "I don't know," I admitted to Rachel's mom. "I just keep God in my heart. I don't need to wait for anyone to tell me what to do with God. I just keep working on building a personal relationship with God, and I trust that he'll listen."

One day, as I was doing some of my typical chores around the house, the phone rang. Picking it up, I found myself speaking to yet another one of my kids' teachers. "I just wanted to let you know, Ali, that Mat's not eating in the cafeteria anymore. He's going out to the bench in the school's courtyard."

"Okay. Is that a problem?" I wondered aloud. Considering the other issues at the school, I wondered if this deserved a phone call home. Maybe I was missing some key detail.

"No, no, not at all. The kids are completely allowed to eat out there—it's just that he's not just out there eating his sack lunch."

"Okay," I said, "what's he doing?"

"He's sitting on the bench and preaching."

"Is that a problem?" I asked again.

"Well, no, I just wanted you to be aware."

"I appreciate that," I assured him. "I'll talk with him about it."

So I asked him, "Your teacher says you've been sitting outside at lunch preaching to kids about Jesus."

"Not Jesus," he corrected. "God."

"You're preaching to them about God?"

He nodded. "I don't know if I'd call it preaching. I'm talking about him. They come with questions, and I try to answer them," he explained.

"Okay, so why are you talking to them about God and not Jesus?"

He nodded as if recognizing my dilemma. "How do you tell someone about Jesus when—" He paused, considering. "It's like math, Mom. How do you tell someone about Jesus when they don't know there's a God? How can they understand multiplication if they don't get addition first?"

# Chapter 19

ONE NIGHT, JAKE found himself in a tall wheat field. The heads of the wheat stalks towered above Jake, their graceful golden stems rising what seemed to be some fifteen or twenty feet from the soil. The sky arched overhead in beautiful tones of orange and blue with the stars visible. A familiar figure stood before Jake. It was the same man that sat on the golden throne that Jake saw earlier. It was God.

Jake stood behind God. Jake reached out his hands and grabbed the right and left edges of his long and sparkling white robes, playing with the hem as he lifted and dropped it up and down again and again, never quite letting it touch the ground. Jake hopped and skipped behind God, never letting go of his robes, enjoying a moment of simple childish pleasure in God's presence. For a moment, the two walked in silence. Jake, an innocent and curious child beside the grandeur of God, never looked away from him.

God's hands stretched out at his sides, broad, powerful, and ancient—so near and large that Jake could see the veins and individual hairs on the backs of them as his fingertips gently brushed across the heads of the wheat tillers like someone pleased with the planting. Jake, let go of God's robes to try and reach the tops of wheat but he came up short. Not being able to touch the top of the wheat, Jake reached back down and grabbed the edge of the robes, once more determined to never let them touch the ground.

Original painting by Cydney in collaboration with
Jake of his vision of God in the wheat fields

They continued to walk with Jake still playfully swishing God's robes up and down with all the innocence and love of a child reunited with his father after being too long apart—and then the atmosphere changed. Jake immediately straightened, his childlike demeanor replaced with a seriousness that matched the question to come.

God solemnly asked, "Is it time?"

Without hesitating, Jake said, "It's time. There is no more good."

God continued to walk, listening.

God's hands fell slowly to his sides, and his pace lessened. Softly, he said, "They are doing it to themselves." Everything went quiet, and a hush fell upon heaven. Then one huge tear fell, and then another, and soon, tears rained down, and Jake felt the power of God's sadness seep into him as it flowed out and filled the air above and the soil below—inescapable and complete. In silence, Jake let go of his robe's hem and continued to walk beside God, feeling God's sorrow like it was his own but larger than he could have ever fathomed. At that moment, Jake finally understood the gravity of God's words, drowning in God's great grief. There was no comfort Jake could give and none he could find.

Jake waited until he and I were alone, driving in the car, to say, "I had another dream."

Seeing how drawn his expression was, how tired and sad, we just drove around, playing sweet music. He described the entire scene to me, giving me the complete dream. He had been like a child speaking earnestly with his father, completely innocent, and then suddenly devastated. If I'd thought Jake was a mess after his first talk with God, hearing God cry as he continued walking down the wheat field's road left Jake an absolute wreck. He was utterly devastated. His sorrow was gut-wrenching.

When he told me what he'd experienced, it was like a stone dropped into my stomach. "Why did you say that?" I asked, shocked. "Why did you tell God to end the world?"

"I don't know," he said. "I saw it, I saw the world forget God and what he has done for us. They worship other gods now."

I was crushed, lost, and still I wasn't as badly wounded as Jake was. I did what was nearly instinctual to me and called Bishop Jensen.

Bishop was flabbergasted. As much as he knew about what we were going through as much as he had tried to offer us assistance in whatever way he thought was appropriate, he was stunned by this newest development. "I don't think anyone's ever heard God cry before," he admitted. "It would be like feeling the pain of the entire world. That's too much for a boy to handle."

Bishop came to the house to talk to Jake, and we all gathered together, listened again, and revisited the emotions of the vision and the ramifications of God's words. With only a few words, Jake spoke the truth that God so desperately wanted to avoid. Jake had expressed God's feelings and the dire warning God gave to Jake was that humanity would decide its own fate, and if humanity continued on the path of abandoning God, mankind would destroy itself.

I wondered if we were doing this for nothing. Why was I fighting so hard when there was nothing *I* could do about it? If mankind was doing it to themselves, then why did I have to suffer? What hope was there? I couldn't tell anybody because people would just think I was nuts, right? Even if I could do something, God made clear that people did not want to be saved. Humanity freely chose to reject God; how many times did people have to push him away before God pushed *us* away?

Jake fell into an even deeper depression and lost himself for a while. He didn't have the same pep or energy—he didn't smile as much. He didn't laugh as easily. I'd drop him off at school, and he could barely make it through the day. I kept getting him for lunch, letting him eat whatever he wanted, mostly Taco Bell. He'd sit in my car and eat his lunch and then go back to school. He needed a break, and I was there to offer a quiet space where he could recoup and recharge.

That feeling of having been in God's presence again and having had contact with something so big and powerful, it was like a drug. It was the biggest high a person could have, and then to be whisked away… Jake missed him and wanted to go back to that feeling, the feeling of peace and love that only God could give.

Jake was still struggling with visions and nightmares and a frequent gut-wrenching nausea from his brushes with evil as it tried to test and lure him, which became a part of normal life. He'd feel sick. His stomach would hurt; his head would hurt. Sleep wasn't as good as it needed to be. There was no clear end in sight, and it was tearing him down. It was just too much for one boy to take.

I'd thought our situation had stabilized after Jake's first talk with God. Things had been far from great, but we had begun to fight back and manage it. But God's crying affected Jake in a way that no evil supernatural being ever could, and its impact was much harder to manage.

One day, as I was preparing to drop Jake off at school, seeing his eyes were red and puffy, I said, "Jake, you don't have to go to school. I can write you a late note."

Jake sucked it up, said, "I'm good," and left the car for school anyhow. I was devastated for him and so outraged at God, the idea that he would put such a weight on my son's shoulders. It was too much.

It seemed like Jake was dying. I would come home after dropping him off at school, crying my eyes out because I could see so much pain reflected in my once playful child's face. He was haggard, worn, suddenly older in a way I didn't like. But every day I had to send him to school, had to let him go his own way without my support for eight long hours and hope for the best. Although Jake was never suicidal, it was as if a light inside of him had been snuffed out, and it was more than I could bear.

Back home, frustrated and helpless, I paced the house for what felt like hours, contemplating what to do. I had never really cared what God might do to me, but I could not handle watching my kid suffer. I dropped to my knees and raised a fist to God, pleading with him, "Can you give him a break? Could you back off just a little? Could you slow down?" I explained to God what was happening to Jake, that he was struggling and facing hardships. I tried to reason with God and ask for guidance.

Having pleaded my case to God, I did my best to place my trust in him and give up any sense of control in exchange for guidance. No matter what he asked, I would follow if he could just give Jake a small reprieve.

How else could I try to fix things? The only religious people we trusted were either moving on or off-limits to our family. The only advice we were going to get, it seemed, came from Bishop, and his advice was always the same: get the kids baptized.

It would be a hard decision and would mean we'd have to go back to the people who censored us, to the people who prevented us from going to the only ward we liked, back to a church that has only caused us trouble.

We never stopped searching for God once we started. Coming from a nonreligious background, neither I nor my family had any idea who God was nor what he could want from Jake. Sure, we knew some of the basics; we at least knew there was a God. Jake gave us undeniable proof of that. From Bishop Jensen, the kids knew there was an ark but did not know who Noah was; they knew Jesus lived but did not know how he lived. We were not getting any help in our discovery to find God or who he was. We began our journey to find

God on our own. We figured if we could find God—if we could understand where and how God originated and how he was first seen and experienced by ancient man—maybe we could find answers to our questions and help for Jake. Our research turned to the book of Enoch, already an ancient story in Jesus's time. It was a book that Jesus would have read and one from which he quoted. The first book of Enoch helped us realize that there was more knowledge of God out there, and it was available to us if we just searched for it.

We started at the beginning and explored history to the time of Jesus and beyond. We wanted to know who God was personally. Of course, we read the Bible, but we went much further. We read about who compiled the books of the Bible, who ordered the Bible to be written, and why certain books were not chosen to be included. Each discovery led to new questions, and each new question was answered with new discoveries. We searched tirelessly on our journey to find God, and through our journey, we learned so many things. The things we learned were things people never learned in the Mormon church.

We continued broadening our understanding of God, studying the Old Testament and then comparing it to the Torah, the Catholic version of the Bible, and the teachings of Greek Orthodoxy. Everywhere we looked, there was more to discover, more to learn.

Late one afternoon, we were spending family time in our backyard, complete with its sweeping view of the city on one side and water on the other. I was chatting with Mat while barbecuing, when I looked over and saw Cydney standing in the door, hesitating to join us, a strange look of fear in her eyes.

She wasn't quite a teen yet, and even though I was well aware of the many bizarre things she'd already experienced, this was odd. She looked like she was frightened to leave the house. "Cydney," I said, looking around and seeing no reason to worry, "come outside."

But she shook her head and said, "I can't. There's a man out there."

I looked around again, puzzled.

"There's a man standing there," she insisted.

Mat and I exchanged a glance. We were less than a dozen feet away from Cydney and saw nothing. "Cydney," I said, "there's nobody here. Come outside." If there was a man outside that we couldn't see, Cydney needed to learn that she didn't need to be afraid. Nothing could physically harm her in any meaningful way. As much as we'd experienced, and as many things had threatened to physically harm us, none of them ever had. Cydney just needed to deal with this. Besides, we were already outside, and surely, we could protect her.

She started crying. "Mom," she said, stricken, "there's a man. Right *there*."

I knelt down and spread my arms wide. "Come on, I'm right here."

Chin quivering, she swallowed hard and stepped outside, the two of us watching her the whole time. She made it two, maybe three steps out before she suddenly stopped. Her body folded into a U-shape as if someone had slugged her in the stomach with a force so great she was lifted into the air. Her arms and legs dangled loosely by her sides a moment before she suddenly dropped to the ground. She began holding her stomach and sobbing, the tears she'd kept inside falling freely. I was stunned, frozen in shock, but Mat crossed the distance in no time, scooped Cydney up, and carried her back inside. I abandoned the barbecue and rushed inside, consumed by guilt.

Mat set her down on the couch. "Are you okay?"

She gave a brave nod through the tears.

"Oh, baby, I'm so sorry," I said, wrapping her in my arms. "I had no idea."

"I told you so," she said fiercely.

"Yes, yes, you did. I'm sorry I didn't realize. I didn't see."

"They shouldn't have been able to hurt you. It was just a spirit of some sort, not something with a physical body," Mat said. "Nothing spiritual has ever hurt us before—" He paused before asking, "Cydney, what did this man look like? What did you see?"

"It was a dark figure, just the shape of a man. He was standing there, watching me." She shuddered. "But it wasn't so much what I saw. I felt nauseated seeing him there. It scared me."

"How do you feel now?" Mat asked, stepping back to look at her.

"Okay, I guess. It took the wind out of me."

In an attempt to better protect our family from things that could now be a physical threat to my family, I started looking even further, consuming everything I could about ghosts and demons, heaven and hell, and all the things in between. What Bishop Jensen told us was not enough; it wasn't working. We needed more answers. We needed information faster so we could fight our enemy. Jensen's church limited him as to what he could do but we did not have the luxury to wait; we had to learn more—now. I dove into an assortment of TV shows, trying to figure out what was legit and what was Hollywood. *Ghost Hunters, Ancient Aliens*—you name it, we gave it a try. Sometimes we learned something useful or that at least resonated with our experiences. Sometimes we were just entertained.

During that three-month period, we were free of nearly all things Mormon. We couldn't attend church at the new ward, even if we wanted to, and we didn't want to go back to the old ward, so we steered clear. Still, my sweet little Cydney's expression of shock and terror when she was attacked haunted me. My baby had been physically struck by something I couldn't even *see*. It only made me wonder about the power of the Holy Spirit even more. Maybe if Cydney had been baptized, she would've been better protected— maybe even untouchable. The idea remained in the back of my head as we focused on hanging out with friends and tried to explain the situation as best as we could while still being careful to not reveal too much. Our Mormon friends were completely freaked out by the way the church was restricting our involvement with it. They'd never seen nor heard of anything like we were experiencing before.

About a year after Jake's first vision, he had a new one in which he woke up in an old church that had been built into a cave. When we, in America, think of old churches, we think of simple construction and buildings that mostly go back to the 1700s. From Jake's description, I knew the "old" he was talking about was in European terms. The building was constructed of a cold gray stone and reminded him of a medieval chapel. As he told me about his vision, I thought back to the stories we'd recently read about early Christians hiding the practices of their faith in caves while people who believed in different deities hunted them.

"There was a hole in the roof," Jake explained, "and in the back of the church were two stained glass windows. Their colors faded. Light entered there and through the hole. That hole looked like something had smashed through it, like a meteor or"—he paused, and his voice grew more serious—"something else. There was a figure inside, someone who seemed almost shriveled and curled in on himself. He was in a shadow, in the fetal position. I could see the top of his head and his shoulders and parts of his legs. I got the sense he was trying to hide in the sanctuary of the church. He was clearly vulnerable, and I knew he was something wrong. Bad. Demonic. But I wasn't scared of him because it was drained of all his energy, all his power. He seemed like a shell of what he had been."

"So he wasn't dangerous?" I asked.

"Not to me. I think, though, that he was what had busted through the roof. When I focused more closely on his form, I realized his skin wasn't so much shriveled as burnt—as if he had been on fire as he fell through the church."

My brain raced from my research. Passages like "And his tail swept away a third of the stars of heaven, and threw them to the earth"; and "I saw a star from heaven which had fallen to the earth; and the key of the bottomless pit was given to him" spun through my head. Could it be?

I shivered, imagining my son being in the same space as a fallen angel—the stars cast down from on high—and it left me with more questions than answers.

# Chapter 20

ONE DAY, A man came to the house, claiming to be an investigator from Mormon headquarters in Salt Lake City. He was neatly dressed and seemed earnest, but I refused to let him inside. He said he had some questions about our situation and what was going on about our case. I replied, "Are you here to help us?"

"Yes," he assured me.

"What do you want to know?"

So while he stood on our doorstep, I explained to him how my children had been denied baptism twice, watching as he took notes. I wasn't sure what I expected, if anything. I really did not care what he thought of us at this point; I was pretty much over anything the Mormons had to say. If he was indeed from Salt Lake, they must've gotten word about the trouble we were dealing with. Maybe they had gotten the letter we had written so many months ago. I would have thought after hearing how my children were persecuted, someone would do something about it. At least that was what a decent organization would do.

But after I'd said my piece and he left, we never heard anything about that brief meeting again. Perhaps Salt Lake was as helpful to us as my mother's ward's leaders had been to her when she went to get help for my stepdad's abuse. Maybe the issues with the church turning a blind eye reached all the way to the top.

Some of the habits I developed as a child stuck with me for decades, and running was one of them. Out on a favorite trail with Rico, my Australian shepherd, I heard someone call, "Hello! Ali?"

My hands tightening on Rico's leash, I turned to see who it was. A man stood nearby, smiling at me. "I'm the new bishop."

I'd heard the rumors. After Bishop Jensen had moved on to a new position in the old ward, the ward had shot through one new bishop and was already on to the next guy. Jackmen. "Oh," I said, "nice to meet you."

"I'll get straight to the point: I heard you and your family went to another ward and tried to get baptized, didn't go through with it, and then left the church. What happened?"

Although this conversation was not at all what I had planned when I laced up my sneakers today, I figured I might as well explain things. "We left the church, yes. We wanted our kids to be baptized, but they've been denied baptism twice by you guys, so we're done. We're good, we're not interested anymore."

"I don't know why they would turn the kids down. Mormons don't turn anyone away from baptism, especially kids. Why would they do that?"

*I don't know, you tell me.* "All we wanted was Bishop Jensen to do it for the kids. He was willing, but you wouldn't let us."

"Hey, Ali!" shouted a woman, quickly approaching from my right. She walked up, coming to stand between myself and Jackmen, completely blocking Jackmen from me. I recognized her immediately. Our daughters attended Brownies together, and she'd been over to our house once but only once. She was a divorcee and undeniably shallow. During that single time I'd had her over to the house, she had asked me why I wanted to stay with my husband, Jay. When I'd looked at her, stunned, she'd wondered aloud, "Don't you want more? A nicer house? Better cars? A finer life? I can introduce you to some *serious* millionaires."

I told her, "I'm good. Thanks." And that was the only interaction I had with her.

Completely ignoring Jackmen, as if he wasn't even worth acknowledging, she reached out to me, urging, "Why are you wasting your time with *him*?"

Jackmen remained silent.

She said slowly, "Come with us."

Us? I glanced around. No one else was with her. No one stood beside her, no one was waiting on her, running in place or stretching. She was alone.

"Come on, Ali. Come with us," she demanded.

"Umm… You go on," I said before lying, "I'll catch up with you later." There was no way I intended to follow her anywhere. Jackmen never said a word; he just looked at her with a perplexed expression and watched her leave.

*Well, that was weird.*

Returning my focus to Jackmen and our impromptu chat, I watched him nod as if our chat had never been interrupted at all. "We can make that happen, you know."

"What?"

"Baptism. We can even have Bishop Jensen perform it."

I nodded. "You can get the kids baptized?" I looked him up and down. Was it too good to be true? I wanted so desperately to believe. I needed so badly to know I had prepared my children for dealing with ghosts and demons with every tool possible. Maybe this man could finally give them the protection we'd been told would make a difference. Maybe new leadership was what the ward had needed to get straightened out. "Baptism by Jensen?" I specified, weighing him with my eyes.

"Sure."

I released a long sigh. The lure of baptism tempted me. The supernatural activity in the house had not slowed down, and even though we'd begun to manage this new normal, we still wanted the protection of the Holy Spirit. Maybe it would give us the break we needed.

"Will you return to the church?" he asked.

I'd seen how vicious the church could get. Would I be trading away my family's mental and emotional safety here, on this plane of existence, for spiritual safety? It was a big decision to make. "I'll think about it."

"Excellent. We'll see you on Sunday then."

I called Jensen right away and told him everything that happened. He was in pure panic mode. He asked, "What did you say to him? Don't say another word to him. Let me handle this." After a short pause, he said, "Let's use this opportunity to get them baptized. If the only restriction they were going to do is make you go to that ward, it's better than what they were doing before. Put your trust in me one more time, and I'll make it happen this time."

After so many months steering clear of anything Mormon, we reluctantly went that next Sunday. For a brief time, things went okay. People seemed civil. And why shouldn't they be? We were doing what they wanted us to do. We were following along, being obedient.

The missionaries were allowed to resume administering the additional and mandatory lessons for the children at our house. We were back on track, and baptism seemed an achievable goal. We already had scheduled the next stage of interviews to take place—these would be with the stake missionaries, which were more senior missionaries who would interview the kids to determine if they were worthy of baptism.

Finally. this was going to actually happen! But Cydney had participated in a special reading contest at school and found out shortly before one of our last meetings with the regular missionaries that she'd won two tickets to an ice hockey game featuring the Sharks. She was thrilled! She, of course, wanted to take her dad, leaving me to host the missionaries for another hour or two of instruction for Mat and Jake.

Unfortunately, I wasn't allowed to host them, not as a woman alone. It simply wasn't permitted in the Mormon church. Bishop Jensen called a friend of ours, Ron, the husband of my best friend, Rebecca, and he came to act as a proper Mormon chaperone. Ron was a very serious man, a devout Mormon who didn't believe in any sort of hocus-pocus. He owned a large company and was very logical, not a man given to flights of fancy. He arrived in a suit and tie and sat dutifully with the missionaries and the children as they talked. During their lessons, he got up three times, each time leaving the room to step into the hallway where he would remain, standing for several minutes before returning to his seat.

He didn't appear to be on his phone. He didn't ask for anything: not the bathroom or a glass of water. It was strange.

At the end of the lesson, the missionaries rose and left, and so did Ron. As odd as his behavior was, maybe he was just stretching his legs. There had to be a rational explanation.

One week later, the phone rang, and I was surprised when I recognized the voice on the other end before the speaker introduced himself as Ron. Ron never called me. I talked to Rebecca pretty frequently, but not to him. "I need to talk to you about the kids' most recent lessons with the missionaries," he explained. "Something happened when I was in your home."

"Okay." Ron was a very smart man—a critical thinker—but the voice on the other end of the phone sounded troubled.

"Every time I sat down," he said, "I saw angels on either side of the boys."

Well, okay. That was not what I was expecting, but what *should* I expect? Weirder stuff had happened before.

"Each time I saw that—these beautiful men glowing an ethereal white—I stood up and walked out into your hallway to try and clear my head. I mean, it was so bizarre. I thought I had to be hallucinating for some reason."

He waited a moment before continuing—maybe a moment in which he thought I'd laugh and say, "Definitely!" Only I didn't. So eventually he drew a deep breath and went on.

"The only problem was each time I came back after talking myself out of what I had seen, I saw them again. Two angels on either side of the kids. Ali, they were still there. Four angels were standing and sitting next to the kids the whole night."

I remained silent. What could I say?

"One even had a hand resting on Mat's shoulder," he said, "like a dad or a big brother does to let you know that you aren't alone."

I started to open my mouth—surely I had to say *something*, but he cut me off.

"Believe me or not, Ali," he said brusquely, "I know what I saw, and I'm having a hard time understanding it."

"I believe you," I admitted. "You aren't the first one to say they've seen...something around the boys."

Jackmen and the stake president, Brandon, came by to visit several times, curious about our children. It wasn't normal to be visited at home by men of their position and particularly not at such a stage in the children's investigation into the church. I quickly learned that Jensen had told them about Jake's visions and what we had been experiencing without letting us know he had done so. They were fascinated by the things Jake had seen. What was an already uncomfortable situation was made worse by the fact Jay wasn't present due to his work schedule.

The two of them sat on the couch with the boys, asking question after question. What had Jake seen? What did he think what he'd seen meant? What had Mat read? What had he learned from his reading?

Although they were very supportive of what Jake shared, seemingly agreeing with key points of what he'd seen, being polite, I remained cautious. These were powerful men, and something about their interest concerned me—being burned in the past, I would be stupid not to be wary.

Even more concerning, though, was the fact they were firm in their demand that we were to tell no one else—not anyone—about what Jake had witnessed. They told Jake to go directly to them if anything happened; they wanted to hear about anything and everything immediately. To give up such control worried me, so I didn't give it up.

One day, in our adult Sunday school class, so bored I wanted to die, I stepped out on pretense of taking a quick pee break. Out in the hallway, I spotted Mat walking down the hall, all alone. I headed straight toward him, realizing he was clearly upset.

"Hey there, Mat, what're you doing out here?"

He let out a frustrated sigh and explained that Brandon had been regularly calling him out of class to interrogate him about Jake, Jake's visions, and our family. The grilling had become nearly nonstop. "I see," I said, wrapping an arm around him and giving him a loving squeeze. "Go get your brother and sister and wait in the car."

He nodded, and I headed right for Brandon's office. I knocked on his door, and he welcomed me as I stood there.

I said, "You are not to pull my son or any of my children out of class ever again without me being present." Then I turned around and walked out the door.

Over the course of several visits Jackmen and Brandon had at our home, their attitudes about Jake's visions changed. They came bearing more questions, demanding more specifics. Each time, Jake and Mat fielded their questions and countered their concerns with facts supported by months and months of deep, meaningful, and thorough research.

"Honestly," Jackmen said, "these visions of yours"—he leveled a look at Jake—"have me quite concerned. It sounds like you think you're a prophet."

Jake said, "No."

"The important thing to understand," Jackmen continued, "is that God only sends one prophet at a time to speak to our church. And we know that God has sent one, and he is currently installed at Salt Lake as is proper." What he said did not really make sense; Jake never said he was a prophet nor was he Mormon. Whatever the church was planning could not be good.

"Tell me more about these visions you're having," Jackmen insisted.

Jake was reluctant to tell someone who clearly had bad intentions.

Jackmen pressed him, "How do you know—in these visions— if something's good or bad?"

Jake explained to Jackmen the same sensation he and Cydney had told me about multiple times: the lurking nausea, the strange sensation that something was simply "off" or wrong, the uncanny impression that warned of trouble, and, in Jake's case, the lesson God gave to him regarding how to discern between good and evil.

"I see," Jackmen said. He glanced at Brandon. "Unfortunately," Jackmen explained, "because Jake saw evil in his vision"—referring to the great battle in heaven—"it can't possibly be from God and must be from Satan."

"What?" I was flabbergasted. "No!"

"We believe your son's visions are coming from the devil." Jackmen shrugged indifferently. "It's as we've said, 'What is good is good and evil is evil, and that which is good cannot be evil,'" he declared in a very demeaning way.

Jake began to sink into his chair, slumping over.

Mat put his hand on Jake's knee and, ever the protector, rose to his feet, countering, "Woe unto them that call evil good and good evil, that put darkness for light, and light for darkness, that put bitter for sweet, and sweet for bitter!" Mat had struck back verbally, eloquently citing an even more applicable Bible verse—and one found in the Book of Mormon too—in defense of his brother.

Jackmen reddened, angered by Mat's bold defense. Here was a boy who would not back down and countered every word Jackmen said with on-point Scripture. Man, was Jackmen ticked off by being bested by a boy!

Upset with the completely inappropriate behavior of these church leaders, I asked them to leave.

The missionaries had finally finished the kids' lessons, and regardless of the frustration we'd had at Jackmen's comments regarding the origin of Jake's visions, we were hanging in there, knowing that we were in the right and that the children's baptism date had finally been set. We only had three days to go! We could do this. All that remained was the children's interviews with the stake missionaries, considered elders in the church. The kids were nervous. They had been through a lot and were going to go through their final interview. It was a long time coming, and for the kids, it had been a Herculean task. They had worked so hard and waited so long…and all their efforts were finally coming to fruition. It was an exhausting fight, but it was finally happening.

The evening of the final round of interviews, with a hearty dinner of pork chops and mac and cheese on the table, and my family gathering to eat, the phone rang. Jackmen was on the other end.

"Hi, Ali." Something about his tone was off. "I wanted to let you know"—he let each word roll out gradually—"I was talking with Brandon, and we've made an important decision here. I'm sorry." I heard each word clearly in his voice. "I wanted to let you know your children have been denied baptism until we decide they are worthy."

They had to be kidding. We'd done everything they told us to do, and now they were denying the kids' baptism again for the third time? It was absolutely unacceptable. Wasn't there a saying, "The third time's the charm"? There was nothing charming about this turn of events!

# Chapter 21

"WHAT DO YOU mean they've been denied baptism until they're deemed worthy?"

Jay moved closer to me and the phone I held so he could hear the conversation. I reminded Jackmen, "Tonight's their last interview. The missionaries are already there. Their baptism date is set. They've done everything you asked. Why—"

Jay's eyes locked on mine, and the color in his face began to change—to redden. A vein appeared on his forehead, and he set his jaw.

Through the phone, Jackmen rambled on briefly, but I barely heard him—something about having had lunch with Stake President Brandon and the two of them deciding they needed more proof of the kids' worthiness.

"They're kids," I protested. "How can they *not* be worthy of baptism?"

Jackmen said, "They have to attend church for the full time and all the church classes. Pay their tithe to that ward, and then"—he paused as if it should be no big deal to us—"we'll reevaluate things in a year."

"So," I said, the anger rising inside me, "you're basically saying that we have to do even more, and after a year, you'll judge if the kids are worthy of being baptized?" I was stunned. From the little I knew about most churches, baptism was a given. There were no hoops for a child to jump through in order to receive it. "This"—I worked to find the words beyond the frustration I was feeling— "feels like extortion."

Without another word to me, he hung up.

Shaking in anger and still holding the phone, I told Jay, "They are denying the kids' baptism."

"What?" he whispered, the word cold.

"They say that they want a year from us, and then they'll think about it again."

"What?" Jay's whisper became a roar. "Why would they do that?" he demanded. "The Mormon church—which allows *everyone* to get baptized—is denying them? I've never heard of any church denying children!" Raging, he tore around the kitchen and dining room like he wanted to knock their lights out.

The kids stared at us, piecing things together before slipping quietly away into the family room.

"I'm calling Bishop Jensen," I shouted, dialing as fast as I could. What sort of religion would do such a thing? The kids were innocents, seeking a closer connection to God, and we'd already done everything they'd asked.

Like always, Bishop picked the phone up quickly.

I started to explain, "They denied us again."

Bishop Jensen interrupted me and said, a note of urgency clear in his voice, "Get Jay on the phone."

"Jay." I held the phone out. "Bishop wants to talk to you."

He glared at the phone, distrust clear in his expression, but he crossed the kitchen and put the phone to his ear, snapping out an angry, "Yeah? This is ridiculous. They're just children. They've been called evil. They've been denied baptism three times. What the f——k more do you people want?"

I left them to talk, hoping Bishop could calm Jay back down, and went to find the kids, unsure of what I was going to say when I found them. They were in the family room, kneeling around the coffee table, holding each other's hands. I paused, watching and listening, my angry and pounding heart quieting in their presence. I joined them, kneeling in prayer, wounded.

Even when they were being kept so far from the Holy Spirit by the Mormons, my children were reaching out to God in perfect trust, asking for his help and guidance. They wanted the Holy Ghost so badly and had done everything within their power to earn it.

Furious, I launched back up and into the kitchen.

Jay had already hung up the phone. I dialed Bishop again. "You listen to me, Bishop," I said, "bring the missionaries back to the church. I am going to show these men that my kids are worthy."

"Ali," he said, his tone soft but filled with worry, "what are you doing—"

"They don't have to baptize my kids," I said, enraged at the very idea. "Please do what I ask."

"Okay," Bishop agreed. "Let's do this."

I didn't care what the outcome was. I wanted to demonstrate the undebatable worthiness of my children.

"No," Jay said, "we're not doing this with this church."

Shooting him a look, I said, "It's not about the baptism at this point, it is about showing our children they did nothing wrong, and I want to stick it up those church leaders' asses!"

The kids jumped up with determination on their faces. I grabbed my purse and keys. We were in jeans and T-shirts, Jake was in sweats. We looked almost as rough as we felt. We had never gone to church looking so underdressed—you didn't go that way. But time was of the essence, and a fire burned inside me, insisting now was not the time to get hung up on something as trivial as looks. *Now* was all about action.

Jay's anger switched focus from the church to my stubborn attempt at making the ward's most important men recognize the truth. "No," he insisted, "we are *not* going."

I led the kids out to the car, ignoring him. "Get in," I instructed. We had to do this. Our kids needed this.

Jay continued arguing; I could see his point: he didn't want us to waste any more time and effort on people incapable of seeing our children's value. But I didn't care. I did it out of rage. I wanted them to look at my children's faces and tell them they were not worthy.

"Get in the car," I told him, narrowing my eyes at him.

"No."

Mat came up behind him, grabbed him firmly by the arm, and said, "Dad, let's go."

Rage filled my heart; there was no backing down. We were going to stick that paper showing the kids were worthy in Jackmen's and Brandon's faces.

Jay looked at our oldest son's face and back at my own. With a belligerent sigh, he shrugged Mat off and climbed into the car. "What're you going to do?"

Throwing the car into gear, I promised, "I'm going to show them just how serious we are. We're going to make sure everything we can do toward baptism gets done. If the kids get denied, it won't be because we didn't do everything we should—it won't be because they aren't worthy. It'll be the fault of church leadership, and everyone will know it."

\* \* \* \* \*

At the church, we were met by the two older, more senior missionaries who were originally supposed to do the children's final interviews. My insistence had encouraged Bishop Jensen to, once again, do the best he could by our family. Even the two younger missionaries who had been teaching the kids showed up, crying over the drama we were all being put through.

We sat in the foyer, waiting for the older missionaries to interview each child, against the stake president's wishes. They were going to do the right thing, even if their leader had said they shouldn't. The younger missionaries sat with us, lending quiet support with their presences.

The elder missionaries stepped out of the office they used and called for Mat.

He stood and stepped into the office, the door closing behind them.

The rest of us sat outside, waiting. After about fifteen minutes, the missionaries stepped back out with Mat. They both looked at us, one of them swallowed hard, and the other gave a sigh and a nod—

they were both clearly a little emotional from the content of their interview. As Mat rejoined us, they said, "Cydney?" And she rose and followed them into the office.

More time passed, and then the three of them emerged, and again the missionaries were emotional as a result of what they'd already heard during the Mat's and Cydney's final interviews.

"Jake," the missionaries requested, and Cydney and Jake switched places, Cydney coming to settle beside me while the office door clicked shut once more.

We waited again, and when Jake emerged from the office with the missionaries, the two men were crying, so moved by his words, and they confessed, so confused by why anyone would dream of denying them baptism. "They passed the interview with flying colors," they said between tears. "They are *more* than worthy."

The elder missionaries focused on Jay and me. "Your kids are very special. We've never seen anything like this happen before. Why would anyone want to keep them from the Holy Spirit?" They seemed to have realized how unfair and seemingly random being granted baptism in their ward was now, and it had shaken them. Maybe they understood how trivial their role in the process was when the stake president could deny children of baptism, regardless of what the missionaries said. Baptism was often regarded as something everyone was eligible for, and it was the first step in increasing a church's or ward's membership. It was counterintuitive to lock innocent children out of a holy ritual meant to welcome them into the church community.

One of the elder missionaries stepped forward and, reaching out, held my hands, whispering, "Don't stop fighting."

"We won't," I promised. If we could just get the kids baptized, get them the extra spiritual shield of the Holy Spirit, we could ditch this church and the conniving and manipulative men at its helm.

And then I heard it—the sound of Stake President Brandon's laughter echoing through the church, originating not far from where I stood. "He's here," I whispered, knowing then what I had to do next. "I'm going to give that motherf——ker the paper the missionaries signed, saying the kids are worthy and shove it up Brandon's ass."

The kids looked at me and asked, "What?"

"Umm." Maybe I should have whispered a little more softly. "He's here," I said. "Brandon."

Jay looked at me. "What are we going to do?"

Ignoring his question, I started walking down the hall leading to Brandon's office.

I looked back over my shoulder and called, "Okay, kids, let's go."

Instead of leaving the church, I turned us all toward its interior, and together we headed to the stake president's office where families were seated and waiting in their "Sunday best" to speak to Brandon and prove their worthiness so they could gain their precious Temple Recommend. Without their Recommend, they wouldn't be able to get married in the church, and their families wouldn't be together with them in heaven. It was a big night for them.

All those people dressed to the nines looked up at us skeptically, our seemingly out-of-sorts family, and we sat down among them, Jay and I planting ourselves on two chairs with the kids sitting at our feet on the floor.

We were determined as ever to see things through. My heart beating like a war drum, just like it had when I saved my sister's life from Terry hanging her, I was not backing down. But, as fiercely determined as I was, I had no plan. I just knew I had to react. Brandon was a high-powered attorney. He ruled our stake's church and made waves in the legal realm. Thousands of people listened and obeyed him regularly.

I may not have had the same influence as Brandon, but I had experienced hardships in my life that made me ready for the fight. I remembered spotting an open door across the hall, abandoned my chair, and slipped inside. I picked up my cell phone and dialed Bishop.

I didn't care about the outcome. If we couldn't get the baptism here that they'd worked so hard for, maybe they'd have to go without. Or maybe I'd have to learn how to navigate the social and spiritual requirements at another church.

I really didn't want to do that. As awful as it was, I knew most of the ins and outs of this church and this ward. It was definitely "the devil you know." I wasn't sure if I could handle starting all over from square one.

Bishop Jensen had already called several times on my cell, wanting to know my plan. I told him, "I have no plan, I'm winging it."

He was freaking out on the phone's other end.

"Brandon's here. And I'm going to have a discussion with him."

"Are you kidding me? What are you going to say?"

"I'll figure it out." I was nervous about confronting Brandon. He gloated to the entire world about how rich he was, saying that he would pay $500,000 dollars in tithe, and that was just the 10 percent required, not including all the other money he gave to the church. But my rage overpowered any fear. I did not care about his pedigree or his wealth; he was just another asshole. I was trying to think about what to say when Jensen said, "Ali, you have a gift. I've never in all my life been able to stand up to anyone and make them listen. What you've done up until this point has never been done before. I've never seen such a fighter, and your words can move anybody—I don't care how big, how strong, how wealthy, how intelligent." He paused, letting his words sink in. "You have a blessing from God. That's what we're going to bank on today. You are the advocate of your children. Do what God tells you to do." He paused again. "Ali," he said, "trust your gut" without any trace of doubt in his voice. "It hasn't steered you wrong yet. My wife, Priscilla, and I are going to pray on our knees until we get a call from you."

"Thank you." I knelt on the floor and prayed, feeling a peace and security wash over me with the knowledge my family was far from alone in this fight. Even if Brandon and Jackmen stood against us, Bishop Jensen and the missionaries were on our side and knew we were in the right. How could we *not* be in the right when we wanted baptism to help protect our kids from the actual evil that lurked around us, always threatening? I prayed for strength, courage, and guidance as to what to say. And, when I was done, I returned to my chair to wait.

We waited there until ten-thirty, surrounded by well-dressed Mormons waiting to kiss some butt. At ten-thirty, Stake President Brandon stepped out of his office to survey his domain. Seeing us there, his expression darkened. "I don't recall you being on our appointment book."

I looked him straight in the eyes, knowing everyone in that room was watching, and said loudly and clearly, "We're here so you can explain to these three children why you denied them baptism... again."

# Chapter 22

THE WHOLE ROOM gasped and fell silent. Brandon looked at me, blinking once, the fake smile dropping away from his face. He briefly took in our outfits, and his expression hardened. We were not dressed the way he expected people to be in order to talk with him. Pompous as he was, we had broken several of the cardinal rules he had for church members in his presence, and he was unimpressed. "Then you'll be waiting a long time," he said before turning on his heel and calling one of the nearby waiting couples to follow him into his office.

I settled into my seat. If it was a waiting game he wanted, a waiting game he would get. "Got nowhere else to be," I remarked.

Brandon finally brought us in just before midnight, long after everyone else had gone. "What can I help you with?" he asked. As if he didn't know.

"You're going to tell Mat, Jake, and Cydney why you denied their baptism. They've had all their required missionary lessons." I handed him the papers we had received just hours before, stating my children were worthy. "Clearly, they qualify for baptism."

Each of our children stepped up and stated their belief in God, Jesus, and the Holy Spirit and talked about how badly they wanted to be baptized. It was the most amazing, touching thing I'd ever seen— even Jay grew misty-eyed hearing them. But Brandon didn't care. And that made it as sickening as it was beautiful.

They sat back down, and I looked at him.

Folding his hands together, he said, "No. Here's what we're going to do. One, you'll go to church for one year, under my and Bishop Jackmen's leadership. Two"—he ticked off the numbers with his fingers—"you will tell all of Jake's visions only to me. Three, after one year's time, we will reassess things. If the children are deemed worthy then, we'll baptize them."

"Are you kidding me?" Jay snapped. "This is blackmail!"

Brandon coolly leveled his gaze at Jay and said, "Now, now, we're both attorneys and know that this is not blackmail." The ends of his mouth rose in a faint smile.

"Okay, *extortion*," Jay shouted. "This is extortion! Threatening to withhold the Holy Spirit from kids just so you can control who knows what about Jake's visions? Totally extortion!"

The ends of Brandon's mouth twitched, but he didn't disagree.

I turned and glanced at my children. I stood up. "Get up, kids, we're done." As we were walking out the door, I turned around. "You'll never hear from us again. Don't come looking for us. Don't you dare ever darken our doorstep. We're done with you, and we are done with this church." We walked out of his office in unison and into the silent hallway, having done what we came to do. The church was empty, except for our family and the man we'd just left behind.

Barely a minute later, the slap of his shoes sounded on the floor behind us, and he called out, "Wait, stop! Come back in."

I paused and turned.

"Please," he said, beckoning to us.

With understandable hesitation, we returned.

"Fine," he said. "We'll baptize you, but the boys will never receive the priesthood."

I was so angry I was about to fight back over the priesthood, too, but I froze when Jay suddenly said, "Okay."

Wait. What? I stared at my husband, realizing a deal had just been struck.

"Great," Brandon said. "I'll see you at the baptism."

Stunned, I followed my family out of the church and into the parking lot. Back at our car and still steaming, I turned to Jay and demanded, "Why did you do that?"

"We can fight those battles another day," he said soothingly. "Let's take this win and run with it."

As much as I didn't want to admit it, Jay was right. We had a win. We could fight for more of what the kids deserved another day.

On the way home, I called Bishop. "They're getting baptized," I said, the words somehow unreal after so much struggle.

He cried in joy before we said good night, both of us knowing the race would be on the next morning to get the arrangements finalized and the kids baptized before anyone could change their minds.

We did everything we could, including calling a few friends to share the good news and invite them to the baptism, and Jensen organized the logistics. Everything started coming together. The primary president of our newer ward (a woman who helped organize and educate the children) was so excited by the news of the baptism she wanted to make sure the right robes were laid out, especially because Mat was so tall. Everyone wanted to be part of our upcoming celebration.

The night before the ceremony, Jake woke me at 3:00 a.m., burning up with a fever of 104. He was sick as a dog, crying in misery, his eyes spinning with vertigo. He couldn't walk, could barely stand. I'd never seen him so sick. I gave him some Advil and kept him close all night long, waiting for the fever to break.

The next morning, he was still fevered when he woke up. Mat and Jay looked at him, concerned. "Well," Jay said, "they obviously can't get baptized today."

Mat shook his head, saying, "That's exactly what Satan wants. We need to do this."

"We have time," I insisted. "The ceremony doesn't start until five. Let him sleep."

So we did. An hour before the baptism was supposed to happen, I woke him and looked closely at his eyes. I called Bishop. He was already at the church, preparing for the ceremony. "He's burning up with fever," I explained. "I don't know what to do."

"He's got ghost sickness. I've seen it before," Bishop said. "Get him to the church."

Mat got him dressed and, with Jay's help, they got Jake to the car, and together we drove to the church. We were nearly done with the entire baptism craziness. Soon our kids would be better protected than ever before. It was like a weight lifting off my shoulders. Bishop met us in the parking lot and helped get Jake inside, the men disappearing into one part of the building as Cydney and I went into another room to get her changed into her white robe.

I soon realized as text messages started to *ping* on my phone that our previous ward's primary president, who had been so excited to help with finding good-fitting robes for the kids, had been turned away at the door by Brandon and Jackmen. And she wasn't the only one—so had a bunch of our friends. There was no time for me to fight that battle now, though. I felt time ticking away, and with Brandon and Jackmen so close, there was no guarantee we could see this through unless we got it all done quickly. So we scrambled to find the right robes and emerged to discover that only a few of our friends had successfully pushed their way past the church leaders and inside. Some were still better than none, and I was willing to take every victory I could.

A bit of noise drew my attention to a door through which a group of older men entered. They were all well-dressed and looked a bit emotional by everything that was happening, and together they took seats in the back. Joining us, Bishop explained that they had been bishops in other wards and were there to support us.

"I know this isn't the order we'd normally do this in," Bishop announced, glancing apologetically at Mat, the eldest, "but we're going to baptize Jake first."

There was no argument—Jake needed whatever help the Holy Ghost had to offer, so we gathered by the font, peering down into it as Bishop said the blessing and dunked Jake into the water. When he pulled him back up, there was such a change in him it was nearly miraculous; although he still looked exhausted, he looked healthier! We realized his fever had broken and he could get his feet back under himself again. Whatever had been trying to keep Jake from being baptized had been stopped, and Jake had been completely healed.

The relief that washed over me was immense. Already the power of the Holy Spirit was making a difference. Maybe it was completely worth the fight we'd had to get it for the kids.

Mat followed Jake, and Cydney rounded out the group. As Bishop had promised, he blessed them in the name of God the Father, Jesus Christ, and the Holy Spirit; there was no mention of Joseph Smith—it was just a simple prayer said by a man who truly believed in God. At the ceremony's conclusion, Bishop spoke about the children's worthiness. All the other bishops gathered into a circle and laid their hands on the children's heads in one additional blessing.

After the ceremony wrapped up, we thought the drama was over, and we resumed with a reception at our house. "You're welcome to join us," I told Bishop.

With tears in his eyes, he rested his hand on my shoulder, saying, "Ali, I have never been so weak in my entire life. When you deal with God and you deal with evil, it pulls everything out of you. All I want to do is go home and go to bed." I understood. With that, we hugged and went our separate ways.

The reception wasn't a huge event but did include a few of our friends who weren't allowed to see the baptism itself. We picked up barbecue and celebrated with fun, music, and food. It felt like we'd achieved something nearly insurmountable, and now things could go back to normal.

Kids ran wild and bounced on the trampoline, while Cydney flitted around like a little butterfly with her little friends, declaring she felt somehow lighter now as music and the glow of our firepit filled the night. I headed inside to put together the strawberry shortcake, my girlfriend Rebecca following me to change her son's diaper. She was on the floor with him as I worked nearby in the kitchen, cake and strawberries spread out before me on the counter.

While both of us were occupied, the phone rang. Thinking it was someone calling to wish us congratulations as several already had, I let the call hit the answering machine, allowing the message to be heard by anyone nearby.

Suddenly, the sound of thousands of staticky and garbled voices all jumbled together, talking and calling over each other, filled the air. I ignored it.

But Rebecca froze in the middle of changing her son's diaper and looked up at me, crying out in a panic. "Can't you hear them? Turn it off, turn it off!"

"Hear what?" I asked, scooping more strawberries onto the cake.

She pointed to the answering machine. "Turn it off!" I dashed across the room to stop the message.

I asked, "What's the problem?"

Rebecca said, "It was evil!"

She shook her head, clearly upset, finished with her son's diaper and, with a quick "Let's not talk about this now," went outside.

We ate our cake, and eventually, everybody left. A little after midnight, we were still cleaning up and bringing in dishes and extra food from outside. Food piled up on the kitchen counter, and I focused on putting the leftovers away while Jay and the kids sat around the kitchen island, Cydney in Jay's lap. Everyone was joking and laughing, our spirits greatly lifted by the baptism.

Seeing a number of calls on the answering machine, I pressed play.

I hit the button on the machine, and we heard one from my stepmother, and then, as I was scraping things into a baggie for leftovers, the strange cacophony of voices I'd forgotten about started.

Everything about Cydney changed at the sound of it. Her body stiffened, and her expression fell as she suddenly lost all control, bursting into tears, and sobbing. "Can you hear that? Can you hear what it's saying?"

"No," I said, looking at Jay. It sounded the same as before, just staticky, garbled voices.

But Cydney's eyes were huge and full of fear. "It's clear as day!" Trembling, she clamped her hands over her ears, trying to block out the noise.

Jay's eyes got big, and he stared at her, stunned, and wrapped his arms around her to comfort her. She kept crying—it was like nothing we'd ever seen before.

But our little butterfly was falling to pieces before our eyes. "I hear someone is trying to hurt her...kill her. She keeps screaming. Oh no, she's so scared! Stop it!" she cried. "Help her, Mommy!"

"Get rid of it," Jay shouted. "Get rid of it now!"

In his arms, Cydney was sobbing, saying, "It's from the bad place."

Launching myself at the answering machine, I slammed my hand down on the button, just wanting to turn it off. For a moment, I stared at the now-mute machine. There would be no listening to that strange message ever again, no other chance to decipher or figure it out—but seeing the way Cydney started to calm back down, I realized maybe not solving that particular mystery was for the best. I wondered if we'd pissed something off with the baptism by giving the kids the gift of the Holy Spirit.

It would only be after additional research and understanding that I'd realize the Holy Ghost had always been with us—we just had to ask—that there were no special man-made or church-sanctioned hoops to jump through to earn the Spirit's attention and support. But we didn't know that at that moment; all we knew was that Cydney's night had been ruined by something she could understand—and we couldn't. In the blink of an eye, she'd gone from being free as a butterfly and a gratefully giggly little girl to being nearly broken by a dark presence we couldn't even see or put a name to.

# Chapter 23

WHEN CYDNEY PRAYED, she burned like a fire lit her up from inside. When she and God connected, sweat poured out of her as her temperature spiked. She regularly prayed before bed, entering into something like a meditative state, and it was in moments like this, the Holy Spirit burning white hot within her, that she'd sometimes receive warnings.

Still not quite a teenager, she'd been growing up around supernatural happenings, so even if she was witness to something truly eerie or frightening, Cydney generally had the mental and emotional wherewithal to set it aside for the night and come find me first thing the next morning. So, one day, when she took me aside before breakfast because she'd seen something, I wasn't necessarily surprised. Such occurrences were becoming frustratingly common after all.

"I saw something last night," she said, making sure we were out of Jake's earshot. We were all careful about that—we didn't want to stress Jake unnecessarily since he was having a hard enough time as it was. We figured if we could just deal with the issue on our own, there was no need in further upsetting Jake.

"What was it?"

Carefully and in that soft way of hers, Cydney began, "There was a cave. I walked through it until I saw a gate. As I walked through the gate, I saw an endless pit filled with a sea of red. An innumerable amount of people screaming, thrashing, pushing, pulling, and clawing, desperately trying to get out of the boiling bloody water, and I knew this was their place, and I felt nothing for them. There, in the middle of the…gore…sat a man…on a throne. But it wasn't just any throne," she specified, "not like a pretty royal throne you'd see in a castle. This was made out of stone. He was wearing a dirty and tattered robe. It was really old. I could see the outline of his face. He was very pale and wrinkled. Scarred. He looked straight at me.

Original painting by Cydney of Tick Tock Man's domain in hell

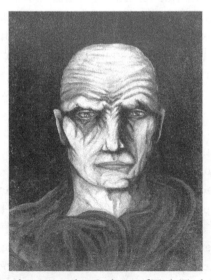

Original painting by Cydney of Tick Tock Man

"He said really slowly, 'Tick tock, tick tock.'" She repeated each word in a carefully calculated rhythm that pushed a chill down my spine. "Your family's running out of time. You will not succeed." She let go of a breath.

"Whoa, creepy," I said.

Cydney smiled, then went about her day as if nothing had happened.

I never told the rest of the family about what Cydney saw. I did not want to unnecessarily upset Mat and Jake. I figured at best it was a nightmare, but more likely, Cydney saw something, and I didn't want to freak the kids out.

But a few days later, Jake approached me. "I saw something," he said. Then he proceeded to tell me, almost in the same words and absolutely with the same sort of description, what Cydney had already told me. Same cave, same throne, same man seated on it.

Now that two of them had seen the same thing, Mat and I conferred about it, flipping pages in a variety of the many different research books we'd gathered. We speculated on it as a family. It was more than a nightmare. And what that being—who Cydney referred to as "Tick Tock Man"—had said was a message we took seriously. We were running out of time? What did that even mean? What did the kids even see? Could it be the watchers from the Book of Enoch, creatures chained deep beneath the earth? Or could it be the bottomless pit that was foretold in the Bible? Was Tick Tock Man telling us the end-times were upon us? Or was it a warning given to Cydney and Jake to become stronger and fight this new threat?

Even after baptism, it was clear that the supernatural activity in our house was not going away. In some ways, it was getting worse. Although we were already adapting to this new level of activity and beginning to manage it, it was exhausting. Jensen, seeing us fight not only at home but at church, suggested we needed even more spiritual power. He thought that the boys should get the Mormon priesthood to further their connection with God and assured us that the priesthood would work to give them yet another layer of protection. He also insisted that even though some people in the church could be wicked, the church itself was true. I wanted to believe that. I wanted to feel like the organization I'd had my children invest time in was a good one, but I had my doubts. How could a good and true organization have such awful people in leadership positions?

A number of weeks later, once again, shortly after Cydney shared that she'd seen and heard Tick Tock stalking through our house, Jake reported something also relating to Tick Tock. There were too many similarities for it to not be the same being. Jake had seen him collecting souls. "I saw him trying to steal souls from God. I saw souls being swayed and taken. He's after God's people."

Bishop Jensen mentioned a new temple was opening nearby and encouraged us to check it out. I had never been inside an actual Mormon temple and had no plans to go into the temple for any service, but, curious, I figured, *Why not check it out before it opens?*

So much fuss was made about attending temple. Attending church (or what some called a "church meetinghouse") was open to almost everyone, but unlike other Christian organizations using "church" and the *concept* of "temple" interchangeably, in the Mormon religion, a temple is a holy building reserved for special services like weddings. You had to have a Temple Recommend to get inside once a temple was officially open for services. And earning a Temple Recommend was nowhere on my to-do list.

So we made the trip as a family to see what a Mormon temple looked like while we were still allowed to enter. Once inside, we were struck by the ornate decoration adorning nearly every surface, but most shocking of all was the temple's massive baptismal font. There was nothing strange about the font itself, but what did disturb us was the foundation on which it rested. Holding it, supporting this vital and primary church ritual, were huge golden bulls. Twelve of them.

Each of the twelve bulls were freshly polished and glistened gold. All twelve bulls formed a circle, and the stone baptismal font rested on their backs. This was where Mormons would bring children and dunk them in the water as a proxy for dead people who were not baptized Mormon, the guide eagerly explained.

Mat was the one who asked, "Why are there golden bulls supporting the baptismal font?"

The guide beamed at us, happy to share. "Well, as you may know, King Solomon was a very wise man, and he had a font designed very much like this one. The bulls were a very important part of it and represent the twelve tribes of Israel. It's as simple as that," he said happily.

"As simple as that," I whispered, visually scouring the temple, examining its every inch, searching for more information. There. I stared at an Eye of Horus. And there, representations of the Greek sun god Apollo. The all-seeing eye of God, the eye of providence, peered out at us too. The mix of symbols was worrisome—why would a Christian church pay homage to the false gods in its inner sanctum? Why would they be present in the temple itself?

We finished the tour but weren't far outside the building when we all heaved sighs of relief. "What did we even walk into?" I said, waving my hands.

They knew what I meant.

"Weird," Jay said.

"Creepy," Cydney suggested.

Mat said, "What's up with the golden bulls? That was creepy." We left feeling very uncomfortable and finding the whole experience strange.

Cydney cornered me again one morning, and just from the look on her face, I knew it was bad. "Tick Tock Man?"

"No," she whispered. Swallowing, she explained slowly, all her typical bubbliness and joy muted beneath a seriousness that made her seem much older than eleven. "I was walking down this hall," she began. "Everything was smooth and cold, soft tones of gray. Like the entire place was made of concrete. It was hard and cold—unforgiving. Someone walked beside me. Glancing at the person, I thought I recognized Mat. I asked him what he was doing there, but he didn't respond. He just kept walking beside me. It was a comfort to know I wasn't alone.

"At the end of the hall was what appeared to be a restaurant. An old man stood by a podium at its front. Even in his suit, he looked way too thin. His face was long and wrinkled, and his eyes were nearly hidden in deep shadows. There were hollows in his sunken cheeks. A thick, red velvet rope separated us from the dinner tables behind him. If we'd been his normal customers, he would have taken down the rope to let us through." She nodded slowly to herself, considering. "I stepped across the rope and headed toward the tables. None of the tables had chairs. But on top of each table was a vase and something that looked like a menu. Only where the restaurant's name might be, or where there might be pictures of the foods they're known for, instead there was a photo of a person and writing underneath it. I leaned closer to read one. Underneath the photo was the person's name and a timeline of the person's life. Each part of their life was outlined with an explanation of their lives, including gruesome details about their deaths.

"I pulled back. I felt a little sick. I said, 'What is this?' The man who'd stood by the podium slowly walked over, really upset I'd gone beyond the velvet rope. Annoyed, he said, 'These are all the people who committed suicide.'"

Cydney looked at me, her big blue eyes soft and steady, and she continued bravely on with the warning. "I looked up," she said, "looked around. The floor, the ceiling, and the walls were all the same tone, all the same smooth, flat, cold, and ungiving concrete. There was no sunlight, no windows. No sense of life or beauty or joy. It was so lonely. So empty. The man repeated, 'This is where those who commit suicide go. You shouldn't be here.' He was really mad. 'This is where the suicides come. This is where *they* belong.'

"I looked down that concrete room that stretched on and on. It seemed endless, table after table lined up and extending further and further into a thick and chilly darkness so deep it was black. There were so many tables, so many places set for people who hadn't arrived. It was ready for so many people, Mom. So *many*."

"Come here." I pulled her to me, squeezing her in reassurance and putting on my brave face. I knew from experience that suicide wasn't always simple. It wasn't always a choice you made without being influenced. I understood too well that sometimes monsters were happily whispering in the ears of struggling people just to see how far they could push them. I also knew those voices could be shut out if you had a strong enough connection to God. If a person only had a chance to think twice and ask themself if it was really them making the decision to die or if it was something else trying to twist their will into doing something awful. If they only had a chance to ask themselves, "Is this really what *I* want?" how many of them would stop themselves from doing something dreadful?

What were all those empty and waiting tables really meant to tell us? That life was going to soon become so hard for so many? That so many monsters were ready to fill a person's ears with poison that all those tables were needed? What was humankind coming up against? And what could we possibly do to help make things better?

With everything happening to us, I would always tell the kids to not concentrate on those things but live in *this* world. Mat and I would secretly investigate it later, but once they told me something, I made it clear—I didn't want them not to think of it ever again, and that's what they did.

Bishop Jensen felt Mat would benefit from having the priesthood, that it would amp up his spiritual power even further. Already a vital protector for our family, giving Mat more power would help him keep everyone safer, so I drove him to meet with Jackmen. As much as I wondered if it would be worth the headaches that were bound to come with getting it, we'd all seen how fast baptism had helped Jake with his illness. Why not get Mat leveled up if we could?

Sitting in a chair in the hallway outside Jackmen's office beside other people waiting to see him, I heard heated voices behind the door and stood, debating whether or not to go in. I rested my hand lightly on the doorknob but stepped back as the door opened.

Mat walked out and as cool as he always managed to be, I knew he was upset. Looking directly at him, I asked, "Is everything okay?"

"No. Jackmen told me that God himself told him not to give me the priesthood. I asked, 'Wait, are you saying *God*?'

"'Yes,' he said, 'maybe in a few days, a few weeks, maybe a few months or a couple of years. When *he* deems me worthy, he will allow me to have it.'

"I told him, 'But you said what's good is good, and what's bad is bad, and that which is good cannot be bad.' So getting the priesthood can only be good for me. Why won't you give me the priesthood?"

I nodded, feeling the heat of everyone's eyes watching us.

The door still open, Jackmen noticed how interested in our conversation everyone else was. He jumped from his chair and pulled us into his office, closing the door behind us.

Inside the office, behind that door, Jackmen sat down, and I proceeded to rip him a new one. I called him a hypocrite, I asked why he needed to bully a child, and I definitely wanted an answer to "Just what the F is your problem?"

As he sat there, glowering, the space between his eyebrows began changing, reddening. It wasn't just a wrinkle or a crease that gained definition there, but an inverted triangle began to take shape between his eyebrows, as if it had been imprinted there. I continued my righteous tirade, watching the strange triangle grow more distinct. Jackmen's expression emptied, the muscles in his face going slack, only the increasingly clear triangle showing that something was happening while time marched on, and I vented my anger at a man who very much deserved my every angry word.

Jackmen had checked out.

It was oddly as if Mat and I were the only two people in the room. I shut my mouth. Standing up, we stepped right up to his desk. Jackmen continued peering into the middle distance. Mat and I got so close to him that I waved my hand in front of Jackmen's eyes, expecting him to blink.

He didn't. There was no flinch, no flicker of recognition or any response.

My skin crawled. This was crazy. As much as something inside me warned me away, I leaned toward Jackmen, calling, "Hello, are you there?"

There was no response.

Shooting me a glance, Mat leaned in too.

In each corner of that bizarre triangle between Jackmen's eyebrows, a small six appeared.

Mat and I looked at the three sixes and slid our gazes to each other. It was so weird. "Well," I said, straightening up.

Mat straightened too.

I shrugged and motioned to the door. Mat followed me out of the office as Jackmen just sat there, staring ahead blankly, the triangle with its three sixes nearly glowing on his forehead. I quietly pulled the door shut behind us. We walked down the hall and stepped into the fresh outdoor air. Barely outside, we turned to each other, and we both pointed to our foreheads.

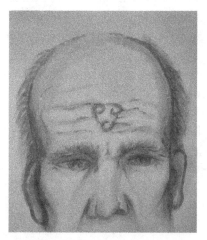

Original drawing by Cydney in collaboration with Ali and Mat of Jackman's forehead imprint of 6s in a triangle

Breathless, I asked Mat, "Did you see that?"

"Those three sixes?"

I shivered, unsure if it was somehow reassuring or even more unsettling that Mat had seen something too. "So weird."

We climbed into the car, and I reached over to the glove compartment and opened it. I yanked out a couple of the standard issue fast-food napkins we always accumulated there and found two pens. I handed Mat a pen and napkin, saying, "Draw what you saw."

He nodded.

I took a pen and napkin and turned so my back was to him. I didn't want to see what he was drawing, and I didn't want him to see my drawing, not yet. We both took a moment to sketch what we'd each seen protruding almost like scar tissue from Jackmen's forehead. "Ready?" I asked after a minute.

"Ready," Mat confirmed.

We showed each other our drawings.

I shuddered. We'd both seen the same exact thing: an inverted triangle with a six forming each corner. Three sixes. My mind went to Revelation 13:18, which stated, "Here is wisdom. Let him that hath understanding count the number of the beast: for it is the number of a man, and his number is six hundred threescore and six."

The three sixes marking Jackmen—one of the two men who had been so intent on keeping my children from getting spiritual protection through baptism and was now trying to deny Mat the priesthood, and one of the two men who wanted control of Jake's visions—was marked with the biblical "number of the beast," the mark of true evil.

Other than being totally freaked out about what we saw on Jackmen's forehead, we never told anyone about it because we thought surely no one would believe us.

# Chapter 24

WE WANTED TO know God as fully as possible, and the church seemed determined to manufacture walls between us. We hungered for a more tangible connection with God. After the fiasco with getting the kids baptized and our desire to see Mat get the priesthood, I became more and more firmly convinced that the power to find and connect with God was within *us*. It had *always* been within us. We didn't need someone telling us what God wanted for us or what God wanted us to do; we just needed to ask him ourselves and listen with an open heart. We desired to see where belief in him started and grew and to connect with him through those places. We decided that the best way to do that was to travel as a family and walk in the footsteps of ancient figures in the Bible.

We wanted to place our feet where Moses walked, pause where Jesus prayed, touch the water where he was baptized. We hoped to grow closer to God by being geographically closer to the people written about in the Bible and other holy books and ancient texts. As much as we believed what Jake had seen, it would be priceless finding his experiences supported in more ancient signs, symbols, and texts. All our studies over the years had allowed us to decide on a list of places we wanted to go, and we knew we wanted to start with Moses in Egypt.

Although the revolution of 2012 had technically ended, Egypt remained politically unstable. In 2011, President Hosni Mubarak had handed power over to the Supreme Council of the Armed Forces, which suspended the Egyptian constitution and disbanded parliament. The military decided to write a new constitution, bring in a new parliament, and hold a new presidential election. When Coptic Christians protested the state-run television channel which appeared to be inciting violence against them, the military opened fire on them and ran some of them down with armored tanks. The military continued seizing power in 2012, and, when elections came, it was a member of the Muslim Brotherhood, Mohamed Morsi, who won.

That was right around the time of Mat's high school graduation. It was then that the travel agent we'd been talking to alerted us to a brief window that was considered a relatively safe time to travel into and through Egypt. Right after Mat's graduation, we packed our bags and flew into Egypt to begin our journey on the trail of Moses. Although it was a dicey time to visit, our desire to learn more about God, and our faith that he would watch over us, led us to hire people capable of keeping us safe. We had someone to meet us at the airport, someone to take us to the hotel, and an armed tourism police officer—provided by the government—as well as several Egyptian guides. The boys were warned to keep their heads down and not look anyone in the eye because they might take it as a challenge. Tensions were high in Egypt, so we balanced curiosity with caution.

Mat brought his Bible, and, as we were going through customs in Cairo, with Jay, Jake, and Cydney leading the way, he was pulled aside as they checked his bag due to something they saw in the X-ray. Pulling out his Bible, they asked, "What is this?"

Mat responded, "It's just a book."

The guy stared at him for a while before saying, "You can go through," signaling us to proceed.

Not all of our guides were male; we had one female Egyptian guide during our first week abroad, and her name was Sara. She led us into mosques, provided us with a copy of the Quran in English, and gave us an entire lesson regarding Muhammad, the Muslims, and their traditions. It was there, thanks to her explanations, that we realized how different our understanding of God was from that of others.

Later that day, Sara took us to the feet of the Sphinx. It was much larger than we thought and looked majestic with two huge pyramids behind it. As we looked at it, we wondered what it must have looked like thousands of years ago in its heyday during the time of Moses. Unfortunately, our time there was interrupted when we heard gunfire erupt. Our tourist police officer led us around the Sphinx's back, hiding us in a small room while he dashed outside. After the shooting died down, our officer returned, moving us swiftly to the van. This was indeed a different world.

Our last day in Cairo, our guide took us to the bazaar. Marveling at all the amazing items for sale, we were barely there thirty minutes when our tourist police officer leaped over to Cydney, put one arm around her, and opened the button on his trench coat, raising his MP-5 submachine gun into the air, and said, "It's time to go!" He picked Cydney up with one arm, carrying her as he rushed us all to the van. Once we were safely inside, he explained two men had begun following Cydney, gradually getting closer and closer to her. One grabbed her shoulder, and he knew then they were trying to kidnap her. Almost as frightening as the threat of kidnapping was the fact none of us had realized it was even happening. Not even Cydney. Being petite, she was used to getting overlooked and pushed around a little in a crowd. It was a busy marketplace and people naturally knocked into one another. It had never occurred to any of us that a bump or a jostle could mean much else.

We left Cairo and rode a riverboat down the Nile, and stopped in Aswan. We were put into buggies, Jay and Cydney in one, me and the boys in another, my sons sitting in front of me to hide me. Pulled by the skinniest horses I'd ever seen, we headed to see the ancient temple, but Jay and Cydney's cart veered away, and we arrived first.

The man in charge of the buggies demanded, "Where is your master?"

Looking at him blankly, I repeated his words.

"He must mean Dad," the boys suggested.

"I don't know," I told him, "one of your guys took him and he is not back yet."

"I want my money. Give me my money!" he shouted.

"I have to wait for my master," I said, playing up to his expectations of a woman relying on her man. Never had I been so aware that all of our money and passports were tucked away in the pouch down *my* shirt. Luckily, Jay and Cydney soon arrived, and things were sorted out. Even though it was a scary situation, we realized how the lack of tourism they so heavily relied on had affected them.

After we finished the river cruise, we flew to the Sinai Peninsula, which was another stop on our spiritual journey. After staying overnighting at the hotel, we readied to start a new day's tour. The heat was oppressive, so Cydney and I wore shorts until our guide sent us back inside to change, explaining that just the day before, an entire American family and their guide had been kidnapped by Bedouins. We needed to cover as much of our skin as possible to make us less obvious. Because of the recent kidnapping, we were escorted into the area by a military truck full of military men.

We journeyed to Gabal Katrine, the highest mountain in Egypt, which was thought in the fourth century to be the Mount Sinai of biblical times. The height of Gabal Katrine was impressive, and allegedly it was where Mosses received the Ten Commandments. We didn't have time to ascend the mountain but wondered what it would be like climb it. At its base, we ventured into St. Catherine's Monastery and walked up to an area with a large bush that had a sign saying it was the location of the burning bush. We didn't feel anything unusual at the site, but it was interesting to think whether we were at the location where Moses talked to God. Since there were few tourists there, we walked into a Greek Orthodox Church, and was able to talk to some of the priests, trying to learn what we could, because, as it says in the Bible in Matthew 7:7–8, "Ask, and it shall be given you; seek, and ye shall find; knock, and it shall be opened unto you: For every one that asketh receiveth; and he that seeketh findeth; and to him that knocketh it shall be opened."

The next stop on our journey was Petra, Jordan, which was a place visited by Moses during his Exodus journey. Like many Americans, we were first introduced to the ancient city through *Indiana Jones*, we were eager to see one of the most famous archaeological sites in the world. It was one of the few places where Eastern and Western traditions met and were truly "carved in stone." We were stunned by the grand and sweeping architectural facades carved into the rose sandstone and excited to explore the area and see if we could find the rock that Moses struck with his staff to draw water. We also learned that this place is where Moses's brother, Aaron, is buried, at Mount Hor. Although we didn't find the rock or where Aaron was buried, it was a magical site and quite breathtaking.

After leaving Petra, our Christian guide, Joseph, wanted to take us to St. George's Church in Madaba, Jordan. He claimed that in the church was an ancient painting featuring Mother Mary holding the baby Jesus. Once a point of pride, it had been protected in a locked metal case with a plexiglass window. He claims one day, a blue hand appeared on the painting, reaching toward both mother and baby. The change occurred without the painting ever being touched and they claimed it was a miracle, Joseph said.

Unfortunately, it was kept hidden in the basement. No one wanted to stir up the idea of one faith having more power than another due to the appearance of a miracle. But Joseph, often bringing visitors to support the church, was allowed to take us into the basement, where he carefully lifted the cloth, the painting was hidden beneath and let us photograph it. Amazing to witness, it left us wondering about the origin of the blue hand. We couldn't find an explanation, but local people declared it was a miracle.

Next, we headed to Mount Nebo, where it was believed Moses ascended the mountain to view Canaan, the promised land, and where some traditions believed he was buried, we met a group of more than a dozen American marines and their chaplain. They were preparing to be baptized in the River Jordan. Hearing English being spoken and an undeniably American accent, Joseph instructed, "Go to your people. Be with your people."

We were delighted to be able to hug, talk, and laugh with these brave young men who were committed to sacrificing so much for the safety of others and wanting to dedicate themselves to God.

As we made our way to visit the site where Jesus was baptized by John, we were struck by both the beauty and the danger of the place. Outside the small pale stone block church on the river's Jordanian side, we were warned, "Don't step off the path" and followed a narrow trail flanked with mines—a reminder that even though Jesus preached peace, people struggle with the concept. The church itself featured a gold-colored dome with a cross topping it. And there, like something out of a movie, sat a live dove. It was perfect.

Nearby, a priest dressed in holy regalia blessed visitors by a huge font. We walked down a few wooden steps to the River Jordan. We could see people being baptized while guards with guns lingered, watching everything. We stuck our feet into the muddy river water and collected some of it in little jars I'd bought earlier, then took the water inside to have it blessed. There was something amazingly beautiful about being there in that remarkable place, which was nearly untouched, other than the mines hidden on either side of the path. It was metaphorically perfect: to find peace and God, you sometimes walked a dangerous path from which you dared not stray.

Our next stop was Israel. On our way into Israel, Joseph said we needed to give him all our documents—our IDs, our passports. We boarded a bus with nothing to our names, not even our luggage. We were nervous because our passports guaranteed we'd get home. "Trust me, and do not look out the windows," Joseph instructed. Holding our breath, we stepped out in faith, handing him everything and not looking outside while waiting for what felt like forever.

Jay said quietly, "Oh shit," putting his hands on top of his head. "I can't believe we gave them all our passports."

Finally, we heard the bus doors open, and a Jordanian soldier got on. He slowly walked down the aisle, staring at each one of us while examining our passports. We were dead quiet, waiting our turn to receive our passports. After we all were given our documents back, we traveled on.

When we got to Israel, we got a new guide named Shmuel, and under his guidance, we toured the holy sites of Jerusalem and Galilee to visit where Jesus taught and traveled. We walked where Jesus walked, taking the path he once did through the Old City of Jerusalem, visited the Holy Sepulchre, seeing Golgotha ("the place of the skull" or Calvary), where Jesus was claimed to be crucified, and even visiting the Garden Tomb where some believe he was buried.

There was an undeniable peace about the garden tomb, between the lush plants in the garden and the graves themselves, allowing it to be a tranquil spot of reflection amid the hustle, bustle, and commercialization of modern Israel.

We flew to Athens, Greece, which was the end of our adventure and last stop before flying home. As our guide waited at our Athens hotel to make sure our check-in went smoothly, he told me, "There's something very special about your children. If you have time, you should travel to Patmos, the island where John wrote the book of Revelation."

Unfortunately, as intriguing as a visit to Patmos where it is believed revelations in the Bible was written, we didn't have any time left to get there.

This trip was our first real adventure searching for God; it opened our eyes to more than just the many books we'd been reading. We visited actual places in the Bible, and it was a trip we would never forget. We visited Egypt where the Israelites were freed, Jordan where Mosses was allegedly buried and where John baptized Jesus in the river Jordan, and Jerusalem where Jesus walked with the cross and was crucified. By visiting these places in history, we made it real, and gave us a new perspective than just words in a book.

But, despite the occasional victory, the longer we stayed in the church, and the worse we were treated—and again and again and by different church leaders—the more they wanted us to obey without question. And the more we wondered why things had to run that way and what was being kept from us, both due to tradition or due to man's desire to control one another. Being told that books outside the church's small list of appropriate reading were forbidden was frustrating. Didn't Luke 8:17 (very much like Mark 4:22) say, "For nothing is hid, that shall not be made manifest; nor *anything* secret, that shall not be known and come to light"?

We discovered during our travels that the church puts God in a small box, but God is so much bigger and greater. If we had stuck to just the short list of books the Mormons allowed, we would never have discovered the amazing knowledge that could be found if one just had the courage to look.

# Chapter 25

IN A DREAM, a voice again challenged me, the message clear: we had to move, leaving our beautiful house and gorgeous backyard with its epic view, ditching the neighborhood and school our kids grew up with and abandoning California. Because something very bad was about to happen.

My heart stubbornly responded with a shout of "No!" I got on my knees and begged, "No, you have to listen. I don't want to move. I don't want to leave all this. If you really want us to move"—my brain ran through the scenarios—"tell Jake exactly what you told me." Yes, that was good; Jake loved it here as much as I did.

We were soon surprised to hear the news that Bishop Jenson had suffered a heart attack. Though alive and recovered, he was not the same man he had been when he played a vital role in our family. To support Bishop Jensen after his heart attack and because he requested it, our family sat with Rebecca's family in the back pew during sacrament. It was then, during prayer, that I opened my eyes briefly and noticed tears streaming down Jake's face. *What the?* Rebecca's eyes popped open, and, seeing him, she looked at me. I focused on the church's front, where Brandon and Jackmen sat. I didn't want to alert them to the fact something was up, but I grabbed Jake's hand and my purse, and we ran outside, jumping into the car. "What's going on, why are you crying?"

He shook his head and said, "Mom, we have to move."

*Crap.*

"I heard the same thing, and I told God to tell you. And since you got the same message, well, sweetheart, we're going to have to go."

"But," he asked, "where will we go?"

"I don't know, but after church, we'll talk to Dad."

None of us wanted to go, but God had other plans. So we took out a map and tried to figure out where to head. We each pointed to different states, discussing our options. In the end, it was between Colorado or Texas. We decided on Colorado since it had mountains.

We bought our Colorado house sight unseen, online. It didn't just have a yard, it had five acres. It was beautiful. Promising.

The school year still not over for Jake and Cydney, we said our goodbyes to Bishop Jensen and his wife and packed up more of our things as Jay and Mat flew out to do a walk-through of the house and accept the keys. Mat called during Jay's walk-through and said, "We won't be living here long."

"Why?" I asked.

"I have a feeling."

No. We were *not* going to move again.

Cydney's and Jake's friends all came over to say their goodbyes, and our yard was full of crying children hugging each other. As much as we'd connected with people over the years, we didn't tell any of them where we were going. God wanted us to leave, so we did our best to make a complete break.

The Colorado house was as beautiful as its pictures claimed. It sprawled across the property, featuring a nearly self-contained basement. Above the basement was the main living space: a kitchen and living room, office, dining room, and master bedroom. On the third floor were the boys' bedrooms. It wasn't perfect—someone had gone overboard with the woodwork, and there was a light in one hallway that blinked on and off at random. And, yes, something about one of the rooms in the basement chilled us, which, with all its exposed cement and machinery, led us to nickname it the "the murder room," but overall, the house was roomy. Gorgeous.

I invited my stepmom over to catch up and help out, and she stayed in the downstairs bedroom that Cydney had rejected. One morning, she complained about the kids knocking on her windows late at night.

"It went on all night long," she said. "I yelled at both Mat and Jake. I even shouted, 'Why are you doing this to me?' They need to stop doing that—it kept me awake."

I knew my kids did not go outside where we had seen bears and coyotes just to knock on the windows. As beautiful as the new house was, something was just a bit off.

While living in our new home, Cydney had another dream. In it, she found herself standing in a dark cave, carrying a torch as her sole source of light. A noise came from the roof of the cave. From the cave's ceiling, a mess of long, wet, black hair swayed, and multiple limbs scrabbled as something crawled down the side of the wall to come face-to-face with Cydney. The creature slowly straightened, standing; its facial features and body shape were feminine. Its flesh was a sickly white, its face partially obscured by long black hair. Two arms were in their normal place, but two arms jutted from the back of its shoulder blades and two more jutted from its lower back. Standing tall, all six arms stretched out as if to grab Cydney, but before it could reach her, she woke up.

When Cydney told Mat and I about the dream the next day, Mat immediately mentioned Dante's work, *The Divine Comedy*. There was a creature fitting Cydney's description in that, but since our copy didn't have pictures, I went to Barnes & Noble and searched for another version of it. Finding one, I paged through it until, seeing a print by Gustave Doré, my breath caught—it was almost exactly as Cydney had described! I brought the illustrated version home, and, showing her the black-and-white image of Arachne, I asked, "Is this what you saw?"

It was, which only supported our belief that Cydney was peering into different realms to warn us about danger lurking nearby—things made of darkness that might be coming for Jake due to his connection to God.

A month into our time in Colorado, and puzzled that no one had come to see us, I drove to the next nearest house to meet the neighbors. "Come in," the woman who answered the door said. "I'm

Trish." Their house was as nice as ours, spacious and well designed, and she grabbed a bottle of water for me from the fridge before leading me to the balcony where her husband sat—a balcony providing a great view of our place. "This is Ali," Trish told her husband. "Her family just moved in," she explained, her gaze traveling meaningfully to our backyard.

"Ah," he said. "Good to meet you, Ali."

"She seems nice," Trish agreed. "Too bad she won't be here long."

Caught off guard, I laughed. "What? No, this is my forever home."

"No, it's not." She smiled at me. "That house has run through a lot of owners already," she explained coolly. "What will they be," she asked her husband, "the ninth owner in the nine years since it was built?"

Her husband took a sip of his water and nodded solemnly.

"But it's such a nice house."

"The builder even left the house before it was finished. It's a pretty enough house, but something about it makes it a bad home."

I don't really know why. Maybe it was morbid curiosity, but we figured we would give the Mormon church one final chance, to see if the church was truly rotten or if, as Bishop said, it was just the people in the California ward who were bad. We figured participating in a religion was the right thing to do since that's what we had always been told. We were in a different state; maybe Colorado's Mormon church would be different. After three months of living in our new home, we decided to give the local Mormon ward's sacrament church service a try. We went in, sat near the back, and left immediately when service ended, returning the next week to stay a little longer and meeting a few women who seemed nice enough. Laura and Danielle were two who were quick to befriend us.

Then, one day, I was called out of our women's Relief Society meeting to visit the bishop's office. "Welcome to our church," he said. "We're always glad to meet new people, and I like to speak to new arrivals personally. Also, just to let you know, I'm going to call your other ward to see how things with your family went with them."

Shocked, I asked, "Do you normally do that to members of your church? Or visitors?"

He said, "No, not normally. But something tells me we should in this case." He paused. "Your family isn't quite like the people who generally join us."

*Seriously?*

I took a breath. I was infuriated, knowing the other ward would not skip a chance to bad-mouth us. After all, we had dared to challenge their authority, and we did not back down when they called us evil or denied us baptism. "Fine," I said. What else could I do?

Two weeks went by. Things were going well, and we had made a few friends. But then I was called back into the bishop's office. The news was not good. "I talked to Brandon," he explained. "Based on what he said, you may not come back here." He continued, his tone growing firm. "You may not attend services, enter the church, or step foot on the property."

"So you're even denying children—including a thirteen-year-old—the opportunity to go to church and learn about God?"

He nodded his head in affirmation.

I said, "You got it, man" and left.

Regardless of the fact we stopped attending church, somehow the girls I'd met through the new ward tracked us down at home. Our kids started hanging out together, and we had barbecues and bonfires, played loud music, danced, and enjoyed each other's company. We made our new friends into good friends. We had been out of the church for a month when Laura and Danielle started asking questions. Laura mused one day, "There's something unique about your kids." I paused to look at her. "Like, with Jake. There's something just...unique about him, isn't there?"

I shrugged and tried to distract her with something else. But Laura wasn't ready to give up so easily and repeated her assertion. I was tired of avoiding the topic or trying to outmaneuver people when they realized that, yes, my kids were not like everyone else's. I didn't really want to tell anybody about what we had experienced; it was exhausting.

For a while, I was able to maintain my evasive maneuvers. Then Laura called one day and said, "Ali. Danielle and I know something's different about your boys. I've been seeing angels with them. And Ali?"

"Yes?"

"Do any of your children have visions?"

*Shit.*

"We're coming over," she said.

While part of the visit felt like any other, I also knew *they* knew. "There's something unique about Jake," Laura said. "What is it?"

"You tell me."

Her eyes got the tiniest bit bigger, and she said softly, "Does Jake have…dreams?"

"He does," I admitted.

She straightened in her seat. "Are they dreams of God or heaven?"

"Yes."

"Please tell me about them."

It was like a dam burst, and I told them everything—what we'd experienced, what Jake had seen, what we'd learned through our long stretch of research—All of it. "And now," I said, "we've been banned from the church, and we don't really know why."

"What?" The girls were shocked. They couldn't believe it. *That* sort of thing didn't happen in the Mormon church.

Only it did. It had. To us.

Laura decided to call her father, a member of the Seventy, a special section of the Melchizedek Priesthood, and talk to him. Our experiences brought up questions for her, and she hoped he had answers. She began asking him questions about the boys' visions and experiences, and she started also sharing information with us about the Mormon church, their beliefs, some things that were startling and some that were disturbing.

She shared things that were supposed to be kept among the Seventies but that her father had shared with her. They told us of Joseph Smith's connections to the Freemasons and how, when they went to the temple, they had to perform a particular ritual that made them feel uncomfortable. In it, they pretended to slit their own throat and stomach, then chanted in a language they did not know or understand. Weird.

Weirder still, the upper echelon of the church had grand plans for building a special temple, and Laura's father was involved in its construction. The building would be put on a property that the Mormons called Adam-ondi-Ahman, a location in Missouri that they claimed was the garden of Eden. The construction of the temple would, when finished, allow the most powerful and holy men of the Mormon church to call down the devil and seal him away forever. It was a shocking proposal. To imagine men so arrogant as to think they could bind Satan after summoning him? It seemed like a recipe for disaster. Really, what could possibly go wrong with all of that?

It wasn't even something we should have been allowed to know about, but having connections to a Seventy came with special knowledge. There was also a belief expressed that if Mormons did all they were supposed to say and do, they would eventually ascend and be allowed to have multiple wives and become a God or Jesus-type deity on another planet. That was also a surprise to us.

The ward received a new bishop, a very nice, simple man with no aspirations for power or wealth, and he reached out to us, asking if he could visit.

"Are you sure you want to do that?"

"I need to come and see for myself if you people are as bad as your ward claims," he explained.

We did not turn him down. We had done nothing wrong. All we tried to do was learn about God and, by extension, help Jake. After watching our family interact and talking to all of us, he came to the conclusion that the boys were knowledgeable and good kids who just wanted to learn about God. "Can I call Bishop Jensen?" he asked. "I'd like to speak to him."

"Of course." I put the two men in touch, and we learned later that Bishop Jensen, always being honest, told him *everything*.

The new bishop invited us back to the church.

# Chapter 26

ONCE PEOPLE STARTED realizing how much we'd learned about religion and God, they started to come to our house to learn from us. They were especially interested in hearing Mat speak and often came with questions. Laura's husband continued to try and frame all of the boys' experiences in the context of the Book of Mormon, feeling more comfortable thinking about things that way, but he kept coming up short. Meanwhile, more people started reporting they saw angels walking with the boys as they headed to and from sacrament and their other church-related classes.

So in that weird way that was distinctly ours, things were returning to normal. As we continued to make connections, the activity in the house grew worse.

Cydney had taken up sleeping either with us or in her brothers' rooms—they were the only places she felt safe. The light in the hallway kept up its weird flickering, and I kept complaining to Jay that he really needed to fix that short.

As weird as the basement was, it was also where we kept our workout equipment. Although running was one of my favorite ways to burn off stress, it wasn't the only way I tried to keep in shape. One day, as I was going through my workout routine, my back to the glass windows looking out on our backyard, I got the creepy sensation that I was being watched. The hair on the back of my neck rose, and I slowed what I was doing as the feeling of eyes on me increased. But as the goose bumps began to rise on my arms, I knew I'd have to face down whatever was behind me, so I steadied my breathing, ready to face whatever lurked menacingly nearby, and spun around.

A half-dozen deer stepped back from the basement's broad windows, startled by my sudden move, but still staring curiously at me through the glass. I nearly fell over laughing.

We introduced our new friends to the research we'd been doing. At church, we met Ryan, whose interest in the boys worried me at first. He was fascinated with them, especially Mat. But we soon realized he identified with their love of reading and research and eagerly gave Mat additional books from his own broad collection, which included some nearly impossible to find volumes. Some were Mormon and included very strange ideas, like the concept that God lived on a different planet or star called Kolob and that Earth was going to fly across the cosmos to reach Kolob. It was odd but intriguing, and Ryan had us all over to dinner often so we could exchange what we'd all been learning. It was wonderful to have our knowledge appreciated rather than shunned.

The bishop seemed very much to be on our side. He confessed to Jake that he believed he could be some kind of messenger from God. Jake immediately said, "I don't know anything about that." Jake explained he lived life like everyone else, and although he had seen some things, it was no big deal. It was what it was. But our new bishop trusted Jake so much and believed so greatly that Jake was a messenger from God he even disclosed personal information about other members in the church to him and explained how he wished they could be more like Jake. This made Jake incredibly uncomfortable. He didn't want to know this information about people in the church and felt it should be kept strictly confidential.

As we attended church, the bishop recommended that we take temple classes as a way to learn more about the Mormons and what they believed in. He also thought it would be a good idea to get a patriarchal blessing. When we went to the patriarch's house to get the boys' blessings, it was somewhat similar to my experience getting my patriarchal blessing as a girl. When we walked into his office, he greeted us and explained the blessing. He said we would most likely be from the house of Joseph, then listed out, almost like from a checklist, the events the kids would follow. He recorded the session, laid his hands on Mat's head first, but struggled to find his words. He paused, then he began to speak and repeat exactly what he said earlier in the order he had said it for both kids, which seemed really odd.

Jake and Mat were also confused when the patriarch said they belonged to a tribe of Israel, when we knew we had no Jewish ancestors.

When Mat got home, he came to us with a Bible and said, "I was reading the book of Revelation, and look at what I found in chapter three, verse nine, 'Behold, I will make them of the synagogue of Satan, which say they are Jews and are not but do lie.'" He looked at me and asked, "Are they really saying we're Jews when we're not?" He ran his finger along the entire passage. "Does this mean they're the church of Satan?"

What Mat read was pretty compelling. Why would the Mormons say we were Jews when we were not? Could they really be the very same church mentioned in Revelation? I'm sure there are plenty of good people in the church—they'd know if it was going down the wrong path. They'd do something. Wouldn't they?

The patriarchal blessing and temple classes and their teachings only served to raise more questions in our minds, and when Mat started asking difficult questions, the church leadership began to take notice.

Our new bishop called Mat into his office and told him, "We want you to go on a mission."

Mat said, "I would like to focus on my education."

"But you're a Mormon, this is what young Mormon men do at your age."

"It's my choice, and I think it's important to go to school," Mat said.

"You are to do what the prophet tells you to do."

"I don't think so."

The bishop next called Jake in and gave him the same news.

"Well," Jake said, "I'll have to consult with God."

"I've already consulted with God," the bishop said, "and he says you're going."

Jake shook his head. "It's between me and God, not me and you."

"No, it's between you and the prophet, and the prophet says you should do it."

"No," Jake said calmly and politely, "it's between me and God."

While we were taking temple classes, Laura started an investigation into why our children had been denied baptism and harassed in all the ways they had. She could not let it go, this idea that her church could be so cruel. And to children! She reached out to her father, a member of the revered Seventies, a higher level of priesthood considered to be equal to the church's Quorum of the Twelve Apostles, both of which had power over the stakes and their wards. Wheels started turning. She and Danielle and others raised questions that made leadership uncomfortable. The letter that Jay and Bishop Jensen had sent to Salt Lake months before had also made it to the new stake president. He was mad that we had not gone to him first, even though we had written the letter before leaving California. Between the letter, the questions raised by my girlfriends, word of Jake's visions, Mat's questions, and the boys' disinterest in going on a mission, it signaled the beginning of the end of our connection to the Mormon church.

A representative from the stake started attending temple classes, and when Mat raised a question the teacher didn't have an answer for, the stake rep tried his hand at providing an answer. When even that failed to provide answers, the stake rep tried to shut Mat down. Jay started sitting in with Mat to try and reduce the censorship, but things were escalating.

We soon learned that the Mormon church leaders wanted to talk to Jake. They extended an invitation to our family to visit Salt Lake City. It was the moment we were waiting for since Jay and Bishop first wrote the letter. From what I'd learned about the Mormon church, they claimed to have a prophet who talked to God. If that was true, I had hoped maybe they could help Jake. Unfortunately, I'd learned, after going through the hell we went through in the Mormon church, there was no way they could help us. It was time to end our involvement with them for good. We began by declining their invitation to Salt Lake. That did not make them happy.

It was during our time in Colorado that I started to really think about writing this book, even though Jake had been telling me since California that God told him that I needed to write everything down. I'd been keeping notes about the supernatural events we'd experienced and what we'd been learning as we went. We knew in our hearts that what we were experiencing was meant to help others too. We just needed to get the word out. A book about all of it could do that. Jake pestered me pretty frequently about writing the book, but it wasn't easy. To help with the process, I purchased a huge presentation-type notepad, covering its pages in sticky notes, each of them featuring something I knew I wanted to include. When I wasn't actively planning or writing, I hung the notepad on the living room's doorknob.

More unusual things started happening in the house.

We heard each other's voices calling for us when we knew the person calling wasn't home or wasn't in the area the voice was coming from. Shadow figures would walk across doorways and down the hall; footsteps sounded where none of us was walking. These occurrences grew more frequent and intense.

The bedroom Jay and I slept in was one of mammoth proportions with a large walk-in closet essentially down a hall but still part of the master suite. Like we did in California, the kids decided to sleep in the closet to get a good night's sleep.

One evening, as I was in the kitchen with Cydney, getting her ready for school the next day, I heard Jay call my name. "I'll be there in a minute," I replied. He called my name again, this time more insistently. "In a minute!" But he called for me again and again, like he had no patience at all. It was frustrating! Clearly there wasn't an emergency. He just wanted my attention, even though he knew I was busy.

Things suddenly jumped off one of the shelves in the living room. But no one was there. No window was open; there was no draft or breeze to explain it. Then my book-in-progress lifted itself off the doorknob where it had been hooked and flew across the room.

Cydney looked at me, and I said, "Right, let's finish this up real quick and head to the bedroom to get Dad."

"Okay, Mommy."

We quickly finished up, and I took her hand, walking past the opening to the living room on our way to the bedroom and ignoring the notebook lying on the floor. "Jay," I asked calmly, "did you call my name?"

Hanging up his towel, he looked at me blankly, his hair damp. "I didn't. I've been in the shower."

"Right."

The light in the hallway of my bedroom flickered.

"Yeah," I said, crossing to the door and pulling it shut.

As we got prepared to go to bed, I heard Jake stomp toward the right side of the closet. "I'm sleeping here." Mat tossed his sleeping bag at the opening of the closet.

"Don't leave me!" Cydney shouted, hurrying to join them. She set her sleeping bag on the left side of the closet.

Shortly after, we went to sleep.

"No, no, no, no, no!" Jake shouted, jumping to his feet.

"What is going on?" I demanded.

"Something keeps grabbing me," Jake explained. "While I was sleeping, I could feel hands tickling my feet. I thought it was Mat, so I kicked a bit but paid it no mind, then the hands moved up to my calf toward my knee, so I threw my blanket at it, but there was nobody there. I decided to go back to sleep, and again I felt the hands move from my feet to my knees. This time, the blanket moved on its own, so I went to look, but the hands kept going to my thighs, and that's when I jumped up screaming."

Seeing the whole thing play out in my head, I barely kept from laughing.

"Then I came in here."

"It happened to me too," Cydney complained.

I have no idea why I decided to do what I did next. Maybe I was just tired, maybe it all seemed too ridiculous to be legit. "Okay, well, how about Jake gets into bed next to Dad, and I'll lie in Jake's spot?"

We switched places, and I got onto Jake's makeshift bed. For a moment, nothing happened, and then I felt the cool brush of fingers by my ankles. They grabbed me, I jerked my leg back, and I leaped up with a "No!" I stomped once and looked at my husband, shocked into laughter. "Jay!" I said. "Something in this room just grabbed my ankles!"

From the other side of the bed, Jake roared, "I told you so, Mom!"

I had met "Casper the Pervy Ghost" and felt every cold fingers and a thumb.

I immediately said a prayer to send it away and climbed back into my bed once I knew things were better.

As soon as school was out, I started interviewing real estate agents. Trish had been right: this wasn't going to be my forever home after all.

We gave away a lot of the things we had just bought for the new house, and I handed Danielle the keys so she could watch the house while we headed to Europe to see what else we could discover. We needed to get out of the States for a while, clear our heads, and see and experience new things. We hopped on a plane and headed off on a new adventure and, en route, bought a new house in another state, also online and sight unseen. But it was brand-new construction, which was—we hoped—a guarantee of no ghosts. We told no one where we were moving to. *No one.* We were learning as we went.

As we traveled Europe, continuing to expand our understanding of God, we occasionally got word from Danielle or the real estate agent about strange happenings occurring in the house. Danielle would often go inside to prepare for a showing and find things from Cydney's shelves thrown onto the floor. She dutifully cleaned them up and put them back, but it was unnerving. Our real estate agent would discover things she knew had been in the cupboard stacked up on the dining room table instead. Whether we were there or not, the house was still entertaining poltergeist-like activity. The house sold, providing us with more than enough money to make our newest leap of faith, and we moved again.

As much as I'd hoped God had sent us to Colorado to truly put down roots, I understood that he sent us there to finish our lessons about some of the more disturbing beliefs held by the Mormon church and to more clearly illustrate the inherent control too often demonstrated by organized religion. In Colorado, I learned our last uncomfortable lessons about the Latter-Day Saints. I finally realized that church was not needed. We never needed guidance on when to pray, fast, bear testimony, or ask for forgiveness. All we needed was a strong personal connection with God.

We'd always had the Holy Spirit with us, and we'd always had God with us throughout our journey too; we just didn't realize or understand it at the time. Our fear of everything strange and frightening going on around us helped keep us in the church. The promise of protection was an immense lure. Besides, it's not easy to walk away from something so many people love and believe in. Instead, it's easy to doubt your interpretation of an organization that holds so much sway over so many people. How can they all be wrong?

Maybe we needed to learn our lessons the way we did: taking our time, questioning everything from God's presence in our lives, to God's ancient connections to humanity, to the true purpose and value of organized religion. Maybe we had to give the church multiple chances to either succeed or fail before we could decide if it was worth our time or effort—if we truly needed organized religion at all. While many people seem to find redeeming qualities in organized religion, we believe firmly that there's a better way for people to connect with God, a way that requires curiosity, lots of questions, lots of research, and lots of thought and prayer, but in the end, it was the best way for us to get closer to God—and that was what truly mattered.

# Chapter 27

THE HOUSE WE moved into was in a nice neighborhood, even if it was a bit too close to a graveyard and, ironically, had Mormon neighbors. We were still searching for a better understanding of God and how he connected to everything Jake had seen and we had experienced—and what it meant for all of humankind. We scheduled FaceTime meetings with people who were considered experts in religious fields, including a rabbi in Los Angeles. He came to a similar conclusion that many other people had: Jake was experiencing God as described in the Old Testament.

The people we talked to, including several rabbis, a Catholic monk, and a biblical scholar, all gave us additional books to read and pointed us forward, on to different places to investigate. They said that many people were searching for something more. Someone with vision and connections—someone they would recognize as receiving messages from God. Some said to keep quiet and not talk about what Jake saw; others said that Jake was a messenger and had a message people needed to hear. Many of these people wanted to meet Jake face-to-face, including the rabbi from Los Angeles, but it was too much, too soon. It scared us. We weren't ready for whatever they had to say.

As much as we hoped to be finished with the strange happenings that so often followed us and just deepen our understanding of God, God had other ideas. Our new home's interior was repainted by a four-man crew, and three weeks after painting concluded, there was a knock at the door. Opening it, I found an older Hispanic man who had been one of our painters, looking down at the hat he held in his hands.

"Can I help you?" I asked.

"Yes, miss," he said humbly. "I had hoped to…be with God again."

Behind me, Jake came down the stairs. "Hello again," he called to the painter, and I realized immediately what the stranger meant.

He had identified in Jake the same thing so many others had before—a sense of peace when he was around Jake—and he wanted to be in that presence again. I couldn't blame him, as strange as his request initially seemed.

Representatives of the Mormon church soon showed up on our doorstep, and we made it clear that we wanted all records tying our family to the church destroyed. We wanted no more connection to their leaders or church.

When our refrigerator started acting oddly, I did what anyone else would and called a repairman. When he arrived, he took interest in the many religious books and artifacts we had in our bookcase. Instead of being a brief visit to fix our refrigerator, it suddenly became a theological discussion when he began talking to me very openly about his issues with religion. "It's frustrating how my church just keeps telling me the same thing," he complained, "as if there's nothing beyond what they repeat all the time. I just feel like there's got to be something more."

I couldn't disagree. I told him if he would like to learn more, he should start by reading the Book of Enoch.

Even in the new couldn't-possibly-be-haunted house, things weren't what most people would consider "normal." Cydney's dreams continued, and she discovered the Gray World, where souls who have lost their way wind up. Dark, filled with caves, and leached of color and life, it was cold and gray and populated by the spirits of those unable to reach heaven: atheists, those who believed in a different god, people who had gotten lost along the way in life, and people unable to face the fact that they died lingered there, too, adrift. It was essentially another unseen dimension, where the population was stuck and hungered for the light that had been denied them. In the dream, Cydney walked to a gothic-looking church surrounded by an iron fence, a broken gate hanging from it. A gravel walkway flanked by graves ran from the gate to the church. There was fresh dirt by the side of one gravestone, as if someone had dug themselves out. Cydney walked past, going to the church's metal doors decorated with a door knocker in the shape of a human head.

Inside the church, a hole in the roof, nearly above the pulpit, spilled a little light into the middle of the church, spotlighting pews that had been thrown around and broken. On the far left, a man in dark gray robes curled in the fetal position, his back against the wall, knees to his chest, his face badly burnt. In that instant, Cydney felt his shame at having been reduced to this and having become something so drained, so small, and she realized he was the one who had dug himself out of the grave.

As a result of all our research, we have come to believe that the Gray World existed in an invisible dimension on this earth. Souls were stuck there in limbo and unable to go to heaven. Many things could invite them into our dimension, such as people engaging in inappropriate behavior, getting into an argument, or bringing a bad presence into their home or lives. The wayward souls yearned for the light of the living and wanted to take it from them.

The next morning, Jake walked into the kitchen, announcing he'd had another dream. In it, he stood on a long beach of gray pebbles and black stones where the ocean only sent small dark waves to lap at the land. He saw three different caves, and, nearby, something that seemed to be a ruin of white marble. Looking to the side, he saw a group of people along the shore, blocking his path. God was there, towering not far away, and with other people standing beside him, who only came to the height of his shoulders. All of them were dressed in white ceremonial robes and white sandals. Jake stood before God as if he was going to be tested in some way. Although he couldn't see God's expression due to the brightness of his face, Jake could sense his mood and knew that whatever it was, it was important.

Instinctively knowing what he had to do, he entered the first cave. It was cold and so dark that he couldn't see anything, not even the walls, the ceiling, or the entrance—not anything. But Jake himself seemed to emit a faint light that acted almost like a shield. Jake closed his eyes and tried to focus. In the dark, something grabbed him. They wrestled. His opponent—whatever it was—was powerful and had a long reach, even managing to nearly put Jake in a head-lock. But Jake got the upper hand and pinned the monster. He was then whisked away from the cave and popped into the next one. This was a spiraling cave of fire, where flames lit pockets in the walls and raced across every surface.

There was an arena—surrounded by a wall of fire—and looking down, Jake realized he held a sword. His opponent had four arms and a flaming sword in each hand. Those arms never stopped moving as the warrior advanced on Jake. Jake parried, blocked, and lunged, countering each attack with one of his own until he had overcome his enemy a moment before he was transported into the next cave.

In the third cave, a half circle of water marked the floor, above which was a ceiling covered in stalactites. Jake walked in the water to the middle of the cave. He heard a deep voice echoing up from the dark bowels of the cave. This time, there was no physical confronta-tion but a debate in which Jake and his opponent argued philosophy and whether or not God had made a mistake and hadn't followed through in the way he should have. Jake argued on behalf of God, explaining that his opponent didn't grasp the full truth or reason behind God's actions. The debate was heated and filled with rap-id-fire responses as the two combatants hurled words at each other, but not in a way that Jake normally used language to communicate. Everything was more abstract, more pointed, and more philosophi-cal. Still, Jake bested his opponent, and God was pleased.

When Jake didn't immediately pop out of that cave and wind up in a new destination, he walked out of it and onto the beach. He approached the ruined marble area where a white marble wall bent around in two opposing half circles, one bending forward and the other rolling back, the marble cracked and written on. Jake peered at it closely, noticing a few familiar symbols that he could not translate before he was transported away again.

He stood on land rolling with patches of green and sand and the rubble of marble buildings. Above the sky was blue, sunny; the day was hot. In one area, huge marble pillars stretched four stories high. A small cracked white slab lay on top.

He walked through two gates toward two marble pillars and noticed a large crater where an impact had hit so hard it was like a bomb had exploded. In the crater's center was a being, hunched into a fetal position, his knees on the ground and forehead in the dirt, his hands covering his long white curly hair and neck in total defeat. He wore a white robe; the muscles of his arms were obvious. His legs were massive. He was strong. Jake knew this being was an enemy of God. Even in defeat, Jake knew the man still had power.

That wasn't the only vision Jake had in the new house. He woke in another vision, kneeling in an ancient and simply decorated gray stone church. Rising, he realized he was alone and wearing a hood over a robe. He heard noise—people arguing outside—like an angry mob. They demanded, "Where is he?"

He opened the doors but, with his hood up, they didn't recognize him and said, "We need to find him." Jake put his head down and walked through the milling and frustrated crowd to ascend a hill a small distance from the church where the tree that had become so familiar in his visions grew. Sitting on the right side of it, he pulled his knees up to his chest, wrapping his arms around his legs and watching the people debate where he'd gone. There, away from everything, Jake found a sense of remarkable and complete peace. Regardless of what happened around him, it seemed to be a place only Jake could go. Below him, he could see a valley between two large mountains.

In the valley, Jake saw a white marble city engulfed in flames. Despite this, sitting underneath the spreading limbs of the tree brought him an undeniable sense of comfort and peace and allowed him to wake up with a sense of calm detachment.

Visions and visitors with strange questions weren't the only things happening in the new house, even though things calmed some after Jake's vision of his trial defending God.

One evening, Jake and I were in the hall after popping some popcorn in the kitchen. We were heading upstairs to the movie room, where we thought Mat, Jay, and Cydney were waiting. We started walking up the house's front staircase when Mat walked right past us, heading downstairs. "Hey," I called, "what are you doing? I thought we were all watching a movie upstairs."

Mat didn't reply, just continued past us and into the office.

We paused, deciding to wait a moment for him. But he didn't return. "Mat?" I called. "What's taking so long?"

On the floor above us, Mat walked out of the movie room and leaned over the railing, saying, "Come on, Mom, it's about to start."

Jake and I looked at each other.

"What the?" I breathed. There was no way Mat could've gotten upstairs without either us seeing him leave the office or coming right past us. This was something new, something I'd never heard of before.

Jake and I ran into the office. There was nobody there.

So I Googled the description of what we'd experienced and learned about doppelgangers. Doppelgangers became frequent visitors at the new house, mimicking each of us. The voices of people who weren't where the voices were coming from also started back up. And so did my Scripture-related cleaning.

That night, I slept with Cydney, and at two in the morning, I heard knocking, and a chill ran through the room. I couldn't help but laugh. It was nuts! I sat up and said, "God, I love you so much, but I need your protection. I need to sleep—I'm so tired."

I heard the sound of canine paws, and my dog—who never slept upstairs—came to my side, gently licked my hand, and lay down at our door, not leaving the entire night. And then, with her on guard, I slept, knowing God had sent her to me.

Even as strange and unsettling as experiences like those were, still, those times were much more peaceful. We, as a family, had been dealing with things like this since Jake had his first vision, after all, and I had dealt with worrying things since I was a child. This was all weird but, generally, nothing new, and certainly nothing we couldn't handle.

I began to think that maybe this was simply our new normal, that maybe we had done almost all God really wanted us to do. I found a sense of peace in that as the kids continued their education, Jay continued working, and I started a business of my own. The world continued to turn, the news grew more worrying, but maybe we'd done everything God wanted us to do already.

One day I was driving my car, my audiobook of the King James Bible playing, and my digital Bible had a weird hiccup. Having just finished playing Matthew 13:43, it skipped back to Matthew 13:37 and went back through to 43.

> He answered and said unto them, He that soweth the good seed is the Son of man; The field is the world; the good seed are the children of the kingdom; but the tares are the children of the wicked one; The enemy that sowed them is the devil; the harvest is the end of the world; and the reapers are the angels. As therefore the tares are gathered and burned in the fire; so shall it be in the end of this world. The Son of man shall send forth his angels, and they shall gather out of his kingdom all things that offend, and them which do iniquity; And shall cast them into a furnace of fire: there shall be wailing and gnashing of teeth. Then shall the righteous shine forth as the sun in the kingdom of their Father. Who hath ears to hear, let him hear. (Matthew 13:37–43)

And it repeated it again and again. No matter what I tried, it kept returning to those verses. And not just that day but for three days in a row. It was unsettling and like God needed me to hear those words in particular—like he needed them to sink in for me, like he was sending a message.

Back at home, Jake came up to me, looking particularly solemn, and said, "Mom, it's time. It's time to write the book."

*Crap.*

With so many people in the world doubting God and turning away from his teachings, it seemed Jake, as he always was, was right once again. So I pulled out my huge notepad, gathered my journals and the resources we'd come to rely on, and got down to the business of writing.

# Chapter 28

GOD WAS NOT done giving Jake visions.

One night, in a vision, Jake found himself seated on a comfortable couch, peering into the distance. Jake watched, surprised as the scene erupted in violence. People before him leaped at each other, fighting, battling with one another, the scene churning with chaos. Horrified, his mind spun, overloaded, as everyone rioted before him, tearing at each other, blood spattering. His brain whirling with what to do, he was transfixed, even as his heart pounded in stress.

Out of the corner of his eye, he saw the figure of a young woman dressed all in white approaching. She sat silently beside him, the couch shifting the slightest bit beneath her. Although he was unable to glimpse her face, she slowly leaned over and rested her head on his shoulder. The chaos, the violence, evaporated, and he let out a gentle sigh. She exuded a comforting feeling that brought him peace. It was a familiar feeling like Jake had when he was in the presence of God. He knew somehow, deep down, that there was no question everything was going to be okay.

Then Jake found himself at another location where, once again, pandemonium broke out, but this time it wasn't localized—it wasn't just in one place but everywhere and even worse. More violence, more rage—there was a frantic intensity to the bloodshed. As Jake considered his options, again the mysterious young woman returned, standing beside him and resting her head on his shoulder. A warmth like the gentlest of the summer's sun seeped into him from her, and he was filled with a sense of serenity that erased all his doubt and worry. He relaxed into that tranquil space, once again at complete peace.

Then, just as suddenly as before, he popped away to another location. Now he stood in the same wheat field where he'd walked with God. Above him, the sky was a beautiful blue as the sun set slowly in the distance. He was no longer a child but a man, and although he was not as tall as God had been, still Jake's hands could brush the top of the wheat as the stalks swayed and leaned to the left, rustling gently in a murmuring breeze. To Jake's left stood the tree that had appeared in so many of his previous visions—a tree representing a pastoral and placid location of calm and vision. Nearby, Jake noticed a few people bending down, examining the golden stalks of wheat. His gaze drifted across the field, soothed by the sight.

Original painting by Cydney in collaboration
with Jake of the tree in heaven

However, Jake identified something different growing in the field, something sticking straight up, fresh and strong, defying the wind. Thinking it might be a weed he should remove, he approached it. Standing before it, he tilted his head, examining it. It was so strange. Slowly he lowered himself onto his knees to take an even closer look. The single stalk was a mix of green and gold, thick and strong with hearty roots and a firm foundation. It did not bend and sway with whatever direction the wind blew. It was more robust than that. So close it nearly brushed his face, the stalk exuded the same warmth and serenity as the girl in white provided. He reached out a tentative hand, curious.

One single and brief touch was all it took for Jake to understand. He jumped to his feet, laughter booming out of him as joy took hold of him. The other people in the field stopped what they were doing and turned to look in his direction, startled. This new, strong, and vital stalk of wheat showed Jake that, far beyond any doubt, God did indeed have a plan. There was still hope for mankind!

# Epilogue

WE CARRY THAT hope with us every day—the hope that mankind will not be completely destroyed by a heartbroken God but that we can turn it all around if we just reach out and connect to God and each other. We strive to do that in our daily lives, and we hope this book will inspire you to do the same.

Our family has settled in our new neighborhood, Jay and I are still working, Cydney's nearly done with high school, Jake's in college, and Mat recently graduated. Life is never dull for our family! We still experience strange things from time to time, and we gladly talk to people about their faith. We're still looking for signs of God all over the world and in ancient written resources. It's an exciting adventure and one we hope to bring you along on through the podcast we're developing.

Books take time to write, and anyone who's ever written one knows it's not easy, but I persisted as we learned the lessons God kept sending our way. We struggled to understand some lessons, but one of the most important among them was that we must each go on our own journey of discovery to find God, and it does not require a go-between to give us permission to connect with him.

Your ability to connect to God already exists inside you, and you connect through doing good things, talking to him, following him, and following Jesus. If your faith is strong enough, you can handle nearly anything, so we learned to connect often and deeply with the Lord. We recognized early that he is listening and loving, even if he tests you. A lot. Along the way, we each built our own special and unique relationship with God through prayer, reading, and research. We understood the importance of asking big questions and listening and watching carefully for equally important answers.

Organized religion can, unfortunately, create more problems than it solves, and history has proven that people hide entire books of the Bible and change meanings and messages of Scripture to suit political agendas. Organized religion also tends to keep people—and the idea of God—in a box, trying to limit what you read and learn about God. Doesn't the Scripture say that *nothing* is hidden? If you look hard enough, *everything* you want to know is right in front of you. Nothing is hidden. That, we realized, was a promise from God, but insecure and manipulative people hide everything, trying to force others to commit to their agenda. Instead, we chose to read widely and wonder.

Jesus himself asked many questions in the temple as a child.

We encourage you, our readers, to be like Jesus in that too. Ask questions. Seek knowledge and don't doubt God's love for you. Remember Jake's second vision of the wheatfields? There was hope there with the fresh young green and gold stalk he found growing in that soil. There is hope for a new, young, and different world to emerge; we just need to help it grow in faith and goodness while the old wheat is harvested.

Readers may ask if, in hindsight, there are things I would've done differently, if I could. The truth is we had no idea what we were dealing with. As much as we searched for guidance, looking for someone to help us figure things out, there wasn't one person or source that had all the answers. We had another path God wanted us to walk. Sometimes we stumbled along it, trying to find our balance and the right places to set our feet, but luckily, our occasionally stumbling journey brought our family even closer together—with each other and with God and Jesus.

That is what we want for you too: a stronger and deeper relationship with the Lord. Have no doubt—you can build that connection, you can experience that faith and joy that comes with such a bond with God. Asking questions about God and of God is not a weakness. It is perhaps the most worthwhile thing you'll ever do, so learn all you can and be like that new stalk of wheat: strong, independent, and the start of a more hopeful future!

From the Coptic Gospel of Thomas Text:

Jesus said: He who seeks, let him not cease seeking until he finds; and when he finds he will be troubled, and when he is troubled he will be amazed, and he will reign over them all.

# About the Author

WHEREAS SOME PEOPLE write a book after getting a college degree on the subject, that's not my story. The school I attended to become an expert was the supernatural school of hard knocks (by unseen hands). I, and my entire family, lived this story and felt every moment of it deeply. Now living in Texas, a devoted mother of three children, loving wife, dog-owner, runner,  and successful businesswoman, I have learned a life's worth of lessons through our battles against the supernatural.

*Heaven Help Us* is my debut book, but I am determined—as we continue on our journey of understanding and watch our recently started social media grow—that my debut will certainly not be my only book.

www.Heaven-Help-Us.com

Printed in the USA
CPSIA information can be obtained
at www.ICGtesting.com
LVHW091559201124
797034LV00002B/256